FINANCING HIGHER EDUCATION

FINANCING HIGHER EDUCATION

Sources and Uses of Funds of Private Colleges in Kerala

E.T. MATHEW

CONCEPT PUBLISHING COMPANY, NEW DELHI 110059

The Indian Council of Social Science Research gave the financial support towards the publication of this work. However, the responsibility for the contents of the book — facts, opinions, conclusion, etc. — is entirely that of the author and not of the ICSSR.

ICSSR Consultant:
P.R. Panchamukhi

ISBN 81-7022-365-2

First Published 1991

Published and Printed by
Concept Publishing Company
A/15-16, Commercial Block, Mohan Garden
New Delhi 110059

Lasertypeset by
Microtech Advance Printing Systems (Pvt.) Ltd.
H-13, Bali Nagar
NEW DELHI 110015

PREFACE

The pre-eminence which Kerala enjoys in the field of education today has been due not only to the enlightened and liberal policies followed in the past by the rulers of the former princely States of Travancore and Cochin, but also to the sustained and tireless efforts of the private sector consisting mainly of the christian churches and community-based organisations like the Nair Service Society and the Sree Narayana Dharma Paripalana Yogam. The high physical quality of life represented by the 'Kerala model' of development is often cited as one of the long-term benefits of the priority given to education. Unfortunately, however, the state of education in Kerala at present is uneviable; the educational ascendancy of the State has become a thing of the past. Gone are the days when individuals, institutions and governments viewed promotion of education as service to society; when teachers, poorly paid and unorganised as they were, yet upheld the profession noble; and when finance did not prove to be an insurmountable stumbling block before a people who volunteered to put in their best efforts to promote all educational endeavours. Education has now turned into a service 'industry'. Private educational managements are unionised; so too are the teachers and the students, of course, on partisan lines. The government foots the bill of salaries of all teachers and nonteaching staff whether they be in the private sector or in the public sector. The public have ceased to get enthused by the promises and pronouncements of the educational agencies and voluntary public contributions to educational efforts have virtually dried up. In the process it is the quality of education which has suffered.

A usual explanation offered for the observed decay in the quality of education is lack of finance. In the present study our effort has been to examine this contention. Our focus is on the financing of higher education in the private sector in Kerala with a view to finding out the extent to which finance constitutes a constraint on its performance.

Collection of data from a sample of 25 colleges was a tedious and time-consuming task. Without financial assistance it would have been impossible to carry out the field investigation and the processing and analysis of data. I express my deep sense of gratitude to the Indian Council of Social Science Research for the liberal financial assistance extended to me for undertaking the project and publication of its results. I also take this opportunity to acknowledge my debt to the University of Kerala for its administrative and organisational support in the execution of the project.

The collection of field data was done by Messrs Joy Thomas, K. Ashraf, K. Jagannathan, B. Gopakumar and C. Raveendran; Messrs V. Prakash and V.S. Ajith provided research assistance. But for the wholehearted cooperation of the principals of the sample colleges, the field data which form the basis for the present study would have remained for more incomplete; special mention should be made of the help received from Professors Abraham Arackal, T.A. George, C.T. Titus, R. Ramachandran Nair and the

Rev. K.C. Mathew – all principals of colleges and Professors M.K. Abraham, L.G. Netto, G.K. Rajendran, S. Vijayakumar, Varghese Mathunny, V.S. Ouseph and G. Karunakaran Pillai, of the Departments of Economics of the affiliated (private) colleges and the University of Kerala. Professor (Mrs.) Kitty Lopez, Deputy Director and the officials of the Department of Collegiate Education, Government of Kerala, also gave unstinted support in the collection of data on government grants to private colleges. I thank them all.

I am specially grateful to Professor P.R. Gopinathan Nair who read an earlier draft of the project report and to Professor P.R. Panchamukhi, the ICSSR consultant, for their detailed comments and valuable suggestions for improvement. Needless to say, for errors which still remain, I am solely responsible.

I appreciate and acknowledge the prompt secretarial assistance received from Mrs. P.V. Ambika and Mrs. S. Usha Kumari of the Department of Economics, University of Kerala and Mrs. D. Girija of the Centre for Development Studies.

E.T. MATHEW

CONTENTS

Preface 5
List of Tables 10

1. Introduction 13
2. Development of College Education in Kerala 21
3. Evolution of College Finances 33
4. Pattern and Trends of Financing of Colleges in the Private Sector: Institutional Sources 53
5. Pattern and Trends of Financing of Colleges in the Private Sector: Non-institutional Sources 80
6. Expenditures of Colleges in the Private Sector: Patterns and Trends 108
7. Performance and Prospect: Interrelationship between Financial and Non-financial Factors 124
8. Summary and Conclusions 149

Index 161

LIST OF TABLES

1.1 Public expenditure (revenue and capital) on education in Kerala for selected years **14**
1.2 Distribution of the sample colleges by region and management **18**
3.1 Tuition fees (Annal) **40**
3.2 Level of operations of the Mar Ivanios College, Trivandrum, 1949-50 to 1958-59 **40**
3.3 Finances of private colleges after the introduction of grant-in-aid code: The case of selected colleges, 1965-66 to 1970-71 **45**
4.1 Institutional financing of selected private colleges in Kerala (average amount per college), 1972-73 to 1985-86 **55**
4.2 Average state government grants of sample colleges, 1972-73 to 1985-86 **58**
4.3 Net grant received from the state government, 1976-77 to 1985-86: Selected colleges **65**
4.4 Average financial assistance per sample college received from the management, 1972-73 to 1985-8669 **69**
4.5 Average financial assistance per sample college received from the University Grants Commission, 1972-73 to 1985-86 **73**
4.6 Average financial assistance per sample college received from the University, 1972-73 to 1985-86 **78**

5.1 Average receipts per sample college from non-institutional sources, 1972-73 to 1985-86 **83**

5.2 Average amount of fees (other than tuition fees) collected per sample college, 1972-73 to 1985-86 **86**

5.3 Average receipts per sample colleges from donations, 1972-73 to 1985-86 **87**

5.4 Donations from staff: Reporting colleges only, 1972-73 to 1985-86 **90**

5.5 Average receipts per sample college from miscellaneous sources, 1972-73 to 1985-86 **93**

5.6 Classification of colleges according to size of donations for appointment of teachers **97**

5.7 Receipts of selected sample colleges from the management for selected years **104**

6.1 Average capital expenditure per sample college, 1972-73 to 1985-86 **111**

6.2 Average yearly capital expenditure of selected colleges, 1972-73 to 1985-86 **113**

6.3 Average annual capital expenditure on laboratory equipment: Selected colleges, 1972-73 to 1985-86 **114**

6.4 Average annual capital expenditure on libraries: selected colleges, 1972-73 to 1985-86 **115**

6.5 Average recurring expenditure per sample college, 1972-73 to 1985-86 **116**

6.6 Average total expenditure per sample college, 1972-73 to 1985-86 **121**

7.1 Performance of sample colleges: Results of Predegree examinations (March-April), 1985 and 1986 **129**

7.2 Ranking of sample colleges with above-average performance: Predegree examination results (average for 1985-86) **131**

7.3 Performance of sample colleges: Results of Degree examinations (March-April), 1985 and 1986 **132**

7.4 Ranking of sample colleges with above-average performance: Degree examinations (average for 1985 and 1986) **134**

7.5 Relative performance of sample colleges: Predegree and Degree examinations, 1985 and 1986 **135**

7.6 Performance of sample colleges: Results of Postgraduate examinations (March-April) 1985 and 1986 **137**

7.7 Ranking of sample colleges with above-average performance: Postgraduate examinations (average for 1985 and 1986) **138**

7.8 Quality of the teachers: Ranking of sample colleges (descending order) according to the percentage of teachers with research degrees, 1986-88 **139**

7.9 Interdepartmental distribution of teachers with Ph.Ds: Selected sample colleges, 1986-88 **141**

7.10 Library facilities of the sample colleges as on 31 March 1986 **143**

7.11 Performance and financing of sample colleges **146**

1

INTRODUCTION

Among the striking features of Kerala's economy, the high priority accorded to education is well known. Kerala leads the rest of the economy in literacy and women's education. The literacy rate of Kerala (70.4%) is almost double that of the all-India average. In female literacy, Kerala (65.7%) is far ahead of other States in the Indian Union. Many commentators have argued that it is largely due to the high rate of literacy that the State has achieved significant reductions in fertility and mortality rates.[1] In fact the development experience of Kerala, because of its unique features, has been referred to by some observers as the 'Kerala Model' which is characterised, among other things, by a relatively low state domestic per capita product on the one hand and a high level of physical quality of life on the other. It may be noted that Kerala's per capita net domestic product at current prices in 1984-85 was only Rs.2,076 compared to Rs.4,103 for Punjab and Rs.3,259 for Haryana.

Education has been able to play a key role in the development of this State thanks to the enormous investment that the people and the government of the State willingly made in the sector in a sustained fashion for several decades since the early nineteenth century. In more recent decades the rate of growth of investment in this sector has been still higher. No data are available on the contribution of the private sector to this gigantic effort. An indication of the high rates of growth of investment in education may, however, be obtained from Table 1.1 which shows the amount of public expenditure on education for selected years since 1957-58.

TABLE 1.1: Public Expenditure (Revenue and Capital) on Education in Kerala for Selected Years

(Rs. crores)

1957-58	1965-66	1970-71	1980-81	1985-86	1986-87
9.97	28.37	60.09	216.45	424.79	489.01

Source: Kerala Budget (various years).

We see that over a period of three decades from 1957-58 to 1986-87, Kerala's public expenditure on education has increased 48 times. In fact a major share of the State's developmental expenditure (on revenue account) is now spent on education. The proportion has varied from 40.2 per cent in 1985-86 to 53.3 per cent in 1970-71. In 1986-87, the latest year for which data are available, the proportion was 43.2 per cent.

The fact that public expenditure on education presents only a partial picture of the total effort in the field should not be lost sight of. One of the unique features of the educational infrastructure in Kerala is the predominance of the private sector institutions. The magnificent role played by private agencies in this State in the field of education – primary, secondary and University – is nationally recognised. To begin with, it was the western missionaries and the christian churches which played a pioneering role in establishing schools (of the modern type) in the erstwhile princely states of Travancore and Cochin during the first half of the nineteenth century. William Tobias Ringletaube of the London Missionary Society started a school in Mylaudy in South Travancore (now in Tamil Nadu) in

1806; Benjamin Bailey of the Church Missionary Society founded the first secondary school, then known as grammar school, at Kottayam in 1819. At a much later stage, during the early decades of the twentieth century, other community-based social organisations such as the Sree Narayana Dharma Paripalana Yogam (formed in 1903) and the Nair Service Society (formed in 1914) also made their entry into the field of education as part of an integrated programme to promote the socio-economic development of the two leading communities of Kerala, namely the Ezhavas and the Nairs. From the very beginning the state government adopted a liberal policy of encouraging private initiative and effort in education by extending substantial material and financial assistance; later, during the second half of the nineteenth century a scheme of grants-in-aid for schools in the private sector also was introduced. It is, however, seldom recognised that though the financial assistance which the government extends to educational institutions in the private sector is substantial in terms of the budgetary resources of the state government, such assistance is still inadequate considered in terms of the accepted goals of educational development. In fact a stage has reached when the mobilisation of nonbudgetary sources of finance has to be seriously thought of.

The present study aims at a critical evaluation of the various sources, public and private, available for the financing of colleges in the private sector in Kerala. It may be noted that there has been a phenomenal expansion of educational infrastructure at the college level since the formation of the Kerala State in November 1956. The expansion took place both in the public and the private sectors; however the number of colleges in the private sector increased at a much faster rate than those in the public sector. Between 1956 and 1968, a total of 72 private Arts and Science colleges came to be established in the State which constitutes as much as 43 per cent of the colleges in this category. Since then the growth has considerably slowed down. At present there are 167 Arts and Science colleges in the state out of which 132 are private. The unprecedented expansion in the number of colleges during the past three decades was, it is generally held by educationalists and other experts, accompanied by a qualitative deterioration in standards. In the words of the High Level Committee on Education and Employment appointed by the State Planning Board, "The state of higher education in Kerala today presents a dismal picture. A number of new colleges have sprung up like mushrooms in thatched sheds and rented buildings without the needed physical infrastructure, laboratory equipments or library facilities. Old or new, all the colleges are overcrowded with students to such an extent as to make them unmanageable. The high standards of academic excellence which marked the college teaching community in by-gone days have considerably deteriorated with the introduction of other criteria than merit for the selection of staff in Government colleges and the system of purchasing posts with donations which is rampant in private colleges".[2]

While there has been much open, and often harsh, criticism of the way private colleges have been functioning, no study exists on the financing of private colleges. The present study addresses itself to this task. An attempt is made (1) to identify and evaluate the various sources of finance and the changes in the pattern and trend of financing over time, (2) to examine the changes in the pattern and trend of expenditures with a view to assessing their significance in relation to the realisation of the goals of higher education, and (3) to discuss the relationship, if any, which exists between financing and academic excellence as judged by the qualifications of teachers and examination results.

Since published data on finances of private colleges are almost non-existent, required information was collected through a sample survey of colleges. The attempt met with only partial success since complete data, especially for earlier years, were not available with several colleges. Besides, the cooperation received from the colleges was not uniform. While some colleges readily cooperated, others were unwilling to furnish the information. In several cases the accounts and the registers in respect of receipts and expenditures relating to earlier years could not be traced. In addition to the sample survey, information was also gathered from other sources as well: from official sources, particularly the offices of the Collegiate Education Department of the State Government; through interviews with teachers, educationalists and managements.

As noted earlier, nearly 80 per cent (132 out of a total of 167) of the Arts and Science colleges in the state are in the private sector. A sample of 25 private Arts and Science colleges which forms 19 per cent of the colleges in the private sector has been selected for the study. Care has been taken to make the sample representative by taking into account the regional variations and differences in the type of management. In the selection of the sample the following criteria, namely (1) regional representation, (2) representation of the types of management and (3) representation in terms of the age differences of colleges, have been applied. First, the Malabar region consisting of the northern districts of the state, namely Kasaragod, Cannanore, Wynad, Palghat, Calicut and Malappuram are educationally backward compared to the Travancore-Cochin region consisting of the southern districts. This aspect has been taken into account in the design of the sample. Second, we have distinctly different categories of private educational agencies in Kerala consisting mainly of (1) The christian churches constituting different denominations, (2) The Nair Service Society (NSS), (3) The Sree Narayana Trust (of SNDP Yogam), (4) The Muslim Educational Society (MES), (5) The Devaswom Board and (6) Individual managements represented by local committees or private trusts. The sample represents all the six categories roughly in proportion to the total number in each category. Third, some colleges are relatively older than others. Most of the older colleges have postgraduate departments while the younger ones function as degree colleges. Our sample includes both (Table 1.2).

TABLE 1.2: Distribution of the Sample Colleges by Region and Management

Type of Management	Travancore -Cochin region	Malabar region	Total
I. *Christian Church*			
1. Catholic	6	1	7
2. Orthodox	1	—	1
3. Jacobite	1	—	1
4. Mar Thoma	1	—	1
5. Church of South India	2	—	2
Sub total	11	1	12
II. Nair Service Society	2 1	3	
III. Sree Narayana Trust	2 1	3	
IV. Muslim Educational Society	— 1	1	
V. Devaswom Board	1 —	1	
VI. Individual Managements	2	3	5
Grand Total	18	7	25

Since the selection of the sample colleges has been purposive, doubts may arise as to what extent generalisations can be drawn from the study. This would depend on the type of generalisation we try to make. For example, there are certain aspects of financing such as government grants for the payment of salaries of teaching and nonteaching staff which are based on uniform guidelines. In such cases the purposive selection of colleges does not obviously affect the validity of the generalisation. However, there are other aspects like the quality of teachers appointed, library and laboratory facilities etc., which may vary from college to college. In such cases generalisations cannot be drawn on the basis of the entire sample. Instead, they may be drawn for each subsample based on such factors as type of management, regional location, etc. For instance, it is well known that different educational agencies pursue distinctly different practices in matters like accepting donations for appointments and admissions. Hence one should expect colleges under the same management to follow broadly the same practices. The only exception in this respect consists of colleges run by individual or single managements (as distinguished from corporate managements) which may vary widely from one another.

Outline of the Study

In the next chapter (Ch. 2), the development of college education in the Kerala region is briefly reviewed. In this review the religious, social and regional considerations that motivated the opening of institutions of higher learning are highlighted. Chapter 3 traces the evolution of sources and pattern of financing of the private sector colleges. Originally the colleges began as financially autonomous institutions but have ended up as heavily dependent on the State finances. An analysis of the various sources of receipts of the colleges, their relative importance and pattern and trends, are attempted in Chapters 4 and 5. This part of the analysis has obvious limitations since data on source of funds other than government grants are incomplete and/or underreported. This limitation would not, it is hoped, distort the real situation significantly since it is known that in recent years the lion's share of the receipts of private colleges is accounted for by grants from the state government. Chapter 6 deals with the expenditures of the colleges. Since salaries of the teaching and the nonteaching staff are directly paid by the government, attention is focused on other items such as expenditures on library, laboratory, etc. In Chapter 7 an attempt is made to examine the interrelationship between techniques of financing, quality of teachers and academic performance judged mainly by examination results. The last chapter (Ch. 8) provides a summary of the discussion and draws its major conclusions.

NOTES

1. In 1985, the crude birth rate (CBR) and the crude death rate (CDR) in Kerala were 23.3 and 6.5 respectively. The death rate compares favourably with that of many developed countries (see, Government of Kerala, *Economic Review 1987*, Kerala State Planning Board, Trivandrum, 1988, p.112).
2. High Level Committee on Education and Employment, *Report on Higher Education* (Kerala State Planning Board, Trivandrum, 1984), p.8.

2

DEVELOPMENT OF COLLEGE EDUCATION IN KERALA

Formal and institutionalised education at all levels had its beginnings in Kerala much earlier than in the rest of India. The educational experience of Kerala, with the state and the private agencies playing significant roles in initiating and sustaining rapid expansion of the education sector, has earned for it a unique position among the states of the Indian Union. The expansion of college education in Kerala had its beginnings in the second half of the nineteenth century. The process of expansion and the forces which underlay it are briefly reviewed in the following sections.

Development During the Nineteenth Century

Though colleges in the sense in which such institutions are defined and understood today were formed only after 1857 when the Madras University was established, a few institutions of higher learning had existed in Kerala even much earlier. The foremost among them was the Old Seminary at Kottayam referred to as the 'Syrian College' by V. Nagam Aiya, the illustrious author of the *Travancore State Manual*, and several others.[1] The Old Seminary was established in 1813 by Pulikottil Ittoop Ramban with the help of Colonel Munro, the East India Company's Resident, for the training of the priests of the Syrian Church. The Seminary was, however, soon thrown open for secular education and non-Christians were also admitted. In response to an invitation by Munro, the Church Missionary Society (CMS) in England sent Benjamin Bailey to Kottayam in 1817 to take charge of the Syrian College as its first principal. It is pointed out that it was Bailey who introduced English education in a systematic manner for the first time in the erstwhile princely state of Travancore. When in 1836 the Syrian Church severed its connection with the CMS, the institution was moved to a nearby location. The Old Seminary from then on functioned as a theological institution and the 'College' came under the CMS. The institution was upgraded to a second grade college in 1892.

The collaborative endeavour between the state and the private agencies which began with the founding of the CMS college has gained strength in Kerala ever since. In the field of education the direct role which the state played is also seen to have been remarkable. Even as early as 1836, the government of Travancore established an English School[2] (His Highness the Maharaja's Free School) in Trivandrum which was later in 1866 developed into a college, then known as the Maharaja's College. The Government Girls' School at Trivandrum founded in 1864 was raised to a second grade college in 1896. These two institutions are now known as the University College and the College for Women respectively. The Government Sanskrit College, Trivandrum, was established in 1889. The Nagercoil Seminary (now in Tamil Nadu as a result of the reorganisation of states along linguistic lines in 1956) founded by the Rev. C. Mead in 1818 to impart regular English education was raised to a second grade college (The Scott Christian College) in 1893. These five colleges were the earliest to be established in the State of Travancore.

In Cochin, another constituent unit of the present

Kerala State, the earliest college to be established was the Maharaja's College, Ernakulam. Begun first as an elementary English school (in 1845), it became a high school in 1868 and a college in 1875.

Among the colleges started in the Malabar region, the earliest ones were the Zamorin's Guruvayurappan College, Calicut, Victoria College, Palghat, and the Brennen College, Tellicherry. Of these the Zamorin's Guruvayurappan College established in 1879 is the oldest.[3] It was started in 1877 as a school known as "Vidyasala" for the young Rajas under the headmastership of one Mr. C.M. Barrow. In 1879 it was raised to a second grade college and was renamed the Zamorin's College. Since then the name of the college underwent change twice.[4] The Victoria College, Palghat, started in 1866 as a 'rate' school was made a 'local fund' high school in 1871. The high school was elevated to the rank of a college in 1888. The Brennen College, Tellicherry, established about the same time also had its beginning as a school. It owes its inception to E. Brennen, Master Attendant at Tellicherry who died in 1859 leaving Rs.12,000 for the foundation of a school to be called Brennen School. The school was opened in 1862. To begin with it was under the management of the Basel German Mission and was known as the B.G.M. Brennen English School. In 1866 the school was raised to a high school. On the retirement of the Basel mission from the management of the school in 1872 the school was taken over by the government. It became a second grade college in 1890.[5]

It is thus seen that, in all, only eight Arts and Science colleges[6] existed in the region, which now forms Kerala, at the end of the nineteenth century. Out of these only two colleges, namely C.M.S. College, Kottayam, and Guruvayurappan College, Calicut, were in the private sector. Invariably all the colleges had their beginnings as schools and when they were raised to colleges they were made only second grade colleges (the only exception was the University College).

Development During 1900-1947

The process of expansion of college-level education continued to be slow even during the first half of the present century till 1947 when the country attained Independence. It is interesting to note that during the period spanning almost half a century from 1900 only 14 Arts and Science colleges came to be established in Kerala. A marked difference is, however, observed in the relative proportions of government and private colleges as between the two periods. While only two out of a total of eight had been in the private sector during the pre-1900 period, the corresponding proportion for the period 1900-1947 was eleven out of fourteen. Out of the three colleges opened in the public sector, the Government Arts College, Trivandrum, was the outcome of a bifurcation of the already existing Maharaja's College, Trivandrum, into a Science College and an Arts College. The other government colleges established during this period consisted of the Sanskrit college at Tripunithura (1914) and the college at Chittur (1947). The domination of the private sector in the field of college education gained for the first time during this period was the precursor of an explosion in the field of higher education during the subsequent two decades. Out of the eleven colleges started under private management during the period 1900-1947, the Malabar Christian College established in 1907 is the oldest.[7] In the Cochin region the earliest college to be established during this period was the St. Thomas College, Trichur, the first catholic college in Kerala. The college grew out of the St. Thomas School founded in 1886 under the Catholic diocese of Trichur. The school became a full-fledged high school in 1904 and in 1919 it was raised to a second grade college. The Union Christian College, Alwaye, the earliest private college to be established (1921) in the Travancore region was an offshoot of the Madras Christian College, one of the oldest and most reputed colleges in India. Initiative for the founding of the Union Christian College came from a group of dedicated young teachers (hailing from central Travancore) of the Madras Christian College who were "inspired by a vision of the need for a centre of higher education run on cooperative basis by Indian initiative for the imparting of sound knowledge, building of character, spread of spiritual truth and knowledge of God".

The St. Berchman's College, Changanacherry, was opened in 1922.[8] It was followed by the establishment of two other Catholic Colleges in Cochin during this period, namely St. Teresa's College, Ernakulam (1925) which was the first women's college to be opened in the private sector. The period from 1926 to 1943 did not witness the beginning of any new colleges in this region. During 1944-47 quite any few colleges came into existence: the Sacred Heart College, Thevara (1944), the S.D. College,[9] Alleppey (1946), the St. Albert's College, Ernakulam and Sree Kerala Varma College, Trichur (1947). With the establishment of these colleges Ernakulam and Trichur emerged as major centres of college education in Kerala.[10]

Period from 1948 to 1968

As we have already pointed out, the period preceding the attainment of Independence was one of slow growth in the field of higher education. No colleges were opened during the late 1920s and the entire 1930s. The reasons are not far to seek. The economy of the region was in the grip of a major economic depression for most part of the period. The Second World War broke out in 1939. Conditions were thus not favourable for launching new colleges. However, throughout this period there existed considerable excess demand for college admissions including admissions for postgraduate courses. The excess demand was met largely by colleges outside Kerala at centres like Madras, Tiruchirapally, Madurai and Palayamkottah (in the south) and Benaras, Agra, Lucknow and Bombay (in the North). Soon after Independence, efforts began for increasing the college-education facilities with a view to fill the gap of unmet demand. Popular governments of Travancore-Cochin (during 1949-56) and Kerala (since November 1956) took keen interest in restructuring and developing the educational system. During the period 1948-68 there was a tremendous upsurge in the field of college education: the number of colleges went up several fold. A few other factors which facilitated this upsurge may also be noted. In the first place was the formation of the Travancore University (in 1937) which was renamed the Kerala University in 1956 consequent on the formation of the Kerala State. Secondly, the pressure exerted by the major communities in the State, namely Nairs, Ezhavas and Christians, on the government in which they had roughly equal representation, also acted as a contributory factor. The rivalry that existed among the communities in the socio-economic field meant that any concession granted to one community had to be matched by a more or less equal concession to another. Soon the Nair Service Society (NSS), the Sree Narayana Dharma Paripalana Yogam (SNDP), and the christian churches were vying with one another to obtain government sanction to start new colleges. It may be mentioned here that the SNDP Yogam was formed in 1903 under the leadership of Dr. T. Palpu, T.K. Madhavan and Kumaran Asan, all disciples of Sree Narayana Guru, the great social reformer of Kerala and the NSS was formed in 1914 at the initiative of Mannath Padmanabhan for the socio-economic progress of the Ezhava and Nair communities respectively. Besides fighting social evils like untouchability, wasteful ceremonies, etc., these organisations were dedicated to building strong economic foundations for their respective communities using education as a powerful instrument. During the early stages of their efforts in this direction, the NSS and the SNDP Yogam focused their attention on opening new schools as they had to start from scratch. After establishing a network of primary, middle and high schools, they turned, in due course, their attention to starting of colleges. The most opportune moment came with the formation of the Travancore University in 1937, a landmark in the history of higher education in Kerala. Though the NSS, the SNDP Yogam and the management of the Sanatana Vidyasala at Alleppey obtained the section of the state government to start colleges, the actual opening of the colleges by the NSS and the SNDP got delayed by a few years owing to the unprecedented political turmoil which prevailed in Travancore State during the last stages of the Dewanship of Sir C.P. Ramaswamy Iyer who had alienated vast sections of the population. It is thus no accident that in the wake of Independence and the subsequent formation of popular government in Travancore, the NSS and the SNDP were able to establish their first ever colleges in 1948, namely the Mahatma Gandhi College, Trivandrum, and the Sree Narayana College, Quilon, respectively. The initial momentum was so powerful that in quick succession the NSS opened three more colleges, namely the NSS Hindu College, Changanacherry, in 1949, the NSS College, Pandalam, in 1950 and the NSS College for Women, Trivandrum, in 1951. It was owing to the untiring efforts of Mannath Padmanabhan, a leader of uncommon devotion and ability that enabled the NSS to achieve such a rare feat of opening four colleges within a short span of just four years. The consequent financial and organisational strain inflicted on the NSS was so heavy that it had to wait for another ten years (till 1961) to open its next college. Since 1961 the NSS has again established several colleges, four colleges in 1964 itself. Compared to the NSS, the SNDP has proceeded at a slower pace in the establishment of colleges. After opening its first college at Quilon in 1948, the SNDP had to wait till 1961 to found its second college at Cannanore. Since then several colleges have been added including five colleges in a single year (1964). Today the NSS and the S.N. Trust (The SNDP Yogam has entrusted the management of its colleges to a trust specially established for the purpose) are the two largest private corporate managements running Arts and Science colleges in Kerala.

As already pointed out, the period 1948-68 witnessed an expansion in the field of college education in Kerala unsurpassed by any other state. Out of 93 Arts and Science colleges opened during this period, only four were government colleges (leaving out the government evening colleges which do not constitute, strictly speaking, new institutions). Significantly the vast majority of the colleges, 72 in all, were established after the formation of the Kerala State in November 1956. Several factors, it may be noted, contributed to the phenomenal expansion of colleges in Kerala since 1948. To begin with, the entry of the NSS and the SNDP Yogam, each representing a major community, into the field of higher education in a big way heralded an era of rivalry not only between these two communities but among all the communities of the state – Nairs, Ezhavas, Christians – Catholics (Syrian and Latin), Non-Catholics (Orthodox, Mar Thoma and C.S.I.) – and Muslims. In the context of the delicate political balance that existed in the state, the government always took care not to altogether ignore the claims of any one group. Another contributory factor was the introduction in 1964 of the two-year predegree course in the place of the one-year pre university class that existed till then. In favour of this reform it was pointed out that the Japanese experiment of establishing junior colleges as post-high school institutions offering vocational education had proved to be successful. Unfortunately, however, almost all of the colleges opened during this period as junior colleges were later upgraded one after another largely for reasons extraneous to consideration of educational progress. As many as 33 junior colleges were opened in 1964 and 18 in 1965. It may be noted that out of a total of 51 colleges opened during the two-year period 1964-65, all except one were in the private sector. A third factor which contributed to the expansion of colleges during the two decades between 1948 and 1968 was the increasing attention paid by the government to the educationally backward districts.

A noteworthy development in the field of higher education during this period was the emergence of the Muslim Educational Society (MES) dedicated to the cause of promoting college-level education among the Muslims of the state who are educationally backward. The first MES college was established at Mampad in Malappuram district in 1965; it was followed by the establishment of the MES Kalladi College in Mannarghat in 1967 and the MES Asambi College, Vemballoor and the MES college, Ponnani, in 1968.

Period since 1969

Since 1969 there has been a markedly downward trend in the opening of new colleges. In all only 52 colleges were started during 1969-87. The pace was very slow for over a decade from 1969 to 1980 when only 16 new colleges were established. A sudden turning point came during 1981, when as if to make up for the relative lull of the preceding period, as many as 25 colleges were sanctioned. Another 11 colleges were added in 1982. A striking feature of the development during this period has been the opening of a very large number of government colleges in sharp contrast to the practice which had existed till then. Such a departure in policy was primarily the outcome of the wide and severe criticism of the manner in which colleges were run by several private managements. Thus as many as 22 colleges were opened in the public sector during this period.

Another salient feature of the development in the field of college education during the period since 1969 was the attempt made to start colleges in educationally backward and remote areas of the state where private managements were not coming forward to establish colleges. Significantly, out of the 52 colleges opened since 1969, as many as 24 were in the educationally backward northern districts of Kerala consisting of Kasaragod, Cannanore, Wynad, Kozhikode, Palghat and Malappuram.

Since, at present, the state government is responsible for the payment of the entire salary of the teaching and nonteaching staff, no new colleges can be started without government sanction. There has been a realisation, though belated, on the part of the state government in recent years that the state already has too many Arts and Science colleges and that any addition to their existing number would not be in the best interests of the state. It is against this background that since 1982 no more colleges whether in the public or the private sector have been sanctioned. As of now, there is a total of 167 Arts and Science colleges in the state (Government evening colleges are not counted as separate institutions) out of which 132 are in the private sector.

It is evident from the preceding account that the development of higher education (Arts and Science) in Kerala has not consistently been based on any rational criteria. On the other hand, the approach has been most of the time purely *ad hoc*. Needless to say, the development has been inextricably linked with the social, cultural and political developments in the state.

NOTES

1. See, V. Nagam Aiya, *The Travancore State Manual*, Vol.II (Government Press, Trivandrum, 1906), p. 447 and K.V. Eapen, *Church Missionary Society and Education in Kerala* (Kollett Publishers, Kottayam, 1985), pp. 122-126.
2. See V. Nagam Aiya, *op. cit.* When the Raja visited the Nagarcoil English Seminary in 1834, he was so such impressed with the importance of English education that he asked for the services of a competent teacher. Mr. J. Roberts, the headmaster of the Seminary went to Trivandrum at the Raja's invitation and opened an English School. The school was started as a private school but was later in 1836 taken over by the government.
3. See, *Madras District Gazetteers: Malabar and Anjengu* by C.A. Innes edited by F.B. Evans (Superintendent, Government Press, Madras 1908) p. 283, for brief accounts of the Guruvayurappan College and Victoria College.
4. The name "Guruvayurappan" was added in recognition of the generous gift of Rs. 5 lakhs made by the Guruvayur Devaswom to the College in 1952.
5. The above account of the origin of the Brennen College is based on *Kerala District Gazetteer: Kozhikode*, edited by A. Sreedhara Menon (p. 636).
6. Professional Colleges such as medical, engineering, law, education, music, Ayurveda and Homoeopathy and special colleges such as Arabic are left out of the purview of the study.
7. As was the case with the C.M.S. College, Kottayam, the Malabar Christian College was the outcome of Protestant missionary effort. Begun in 1848 as primary school by the Basal Evangelical Mission at Kallai (in Calicut), it became a middle school in 1872 and a high school in 1878.
8. It was probably the establishment of the Union Christian College at Alwaye by the non-Catholic denominations which provided the immediate inspiration for the establishment of the St. Berchman's College, Changanacherry. Inspiration must have come also from the St. Thomas College, Trichur.
9. The S.D. college grew out of the Sanatana Dharma Vidyasala, a renowned high school managed by a company

registered in 1909 under the Companies Act.

10. The liberal educational policy characterised by the sanctioning of a good number of private colleges in Cochin during 1944-47 may be attributed partly to the constitutional reforms introduced in 1938 according to which in addition to the Dewan, members of the legislature numbering four were appointed as ministers to advise the Maharaja, education being one of the subjects transferred to the ministers. See, R. Ramachandran Nair, *Constitutional Experiments in Kerala* (St. Joseph's Press, Trivandrum, 1964), p. 30.

3

EVOLUTION OF COLLEGE FINANCES

Historically speaking, several experiments have gone into the financing of colleges in Kerala. However, the full details of such experiments are not widely known as there exist few published accounts. Except for an occasional brief note on the history of a college (providing an account of the growth of the college in terms of enrolment and the level and number of courses offered) given in its magazines and calendars, there do not exist systematic studies on college finances as such.[1] It is well known that college managements have had to face varying degrees of acute financial stringency especially during the early stages. It is, however, impossible in a study such as the present one to give an exhaustive treatment of the processes, problems, and patterns of financing of college education in Kerala. What is attempted below and in the chapters which follow is only a limited review. It is hoped that such a limited effort will encourage further studies in the field.

Initial Capital Expenditures

The first requirement to be fulfilled by a management in the establishment of a college is the provision of a minimum prescribed extent of land.[2] Next in importance is the availability of sufficient number of rooms of suitable size to accommodate the classes and the staff. And finally norms regarding library and laboratories have to be satisfied. Since the size and the number of laboratories required depend upon the courses started and the number of students admitted to each course, expenditure on this item is usually undertaken in a phased manner. The same is more or less true of expenditure on library too.

The early history of colleges in Kerala shows that there existed broadly three ways of securing land for a college: (1) gift from the state government, (2) gifts from private individuals and (3) purchase by management (financed by donations raised from the public and/or members of the particular community under whose auspices the college was to be started). In earlier days when land was available in plenty and land values low, and colleges were few, the government itself came forward to encourage the establishment of colleges in the private sector with liberal grants of land. As far back as 1813 the land for the Old Seminary (Syrian College) and about quarter of a century later, the CMS College, Kottayam and in very recent times the land for the Mahatma Gandhi College, Trivandrum, and the Sree Narayana College, Quilon, were donated by the government. As noted in the preceding chapter, the Old Seminary at Kottayam was established entirely at the cost of the Travancore Government. Rani Lakshmi Bai of Travancore made a grant of 16 acres of land on the banks of the Meenachil river free of tax and a sum of Rs. 20,000 to the Seminary.[3] When, in the 1830s, the English Missionaries (of the Church missionary Society) fell out with the leadership of the Syrian Church, the missionaries moved out and continued their educational efforts which led to the emergence of the C.M.S. College, Kottayam. In more recent times there have been several instances in which the state government donated the required land for the establishment of colleges. To mention only a few prominent cases, the

Union Christian College, Alwaye, was started in an old *cutchery* (court) building which stood on an 18-acre plot of land donated by the Maharaja of Travancore. Forty-six acres of land at Trivandrum were given in 1948 to the Nair Service Society for the establishment of the Mahatma Gandhi College. In the same year a 30-acre plot at the Cantonment Maidan at Quilon was granted to the S.N.D.P. Yogam for starting the Sree Narayana College, Quilon. These were the first and the premier colleges to be opened by the NSS and the SNDP, two of the leading socio-cultural organisations of the state. A decade and a half later in 1964 the state government made a grant of 26 acres of land for the starting of the Devaswom Board College at Sasthamcotta.

Lands for the establishment of colleges used to come in several instances also from donations by individuals or organisations. In fact several of the colleges now in existence would not have come into existence at all but for the generous gifts of land and funds by magnanimous individuals. For instance, the offer by V.S. Sivarama Krishna Iyer of an amount of Rs. 50,000 enabled the Payyannur Educational Society to purchase 157 acres of hilly land for starting the Payyannur College in 1965. The entire land for the NSS College at Manjeri was donated by P.M. Thirumulpad. The establishment of the S.N. College, Chelannur, was made possible by a gift of 67 acres of land by the Sree Narayana Educational Society of Chelannur.

By and large, however, the lands required for the establishment of colleges in the private sector were acquired with funds raised from the public, mostly from members of the community which sponsored the colleges and to a limited extent from members of other communities. The financial campaign to raise funds for the purchase of land, and subsequently for the construction of the buildings, has in most cases followed a typical pattern. First, a large and representative committee is set up for the purpose;

the members of the committee approach potential donors in small groups with an appeal for funds. Often the appeal was not only for raising funds for the purchase of the land required, but also for the construction of the building immediately required to house the college. A donation list is opened; invariably the list begins with a few large donations running to a few thousands of rupees in order to ensure that other potential donors whose names would follow do not put paltry sums by way of their donations. The extent of the effort required would depend, of course, on the general economic condition of the community or the group which sponsors the college. Nevertheless even organisations like the NSS and the SN Trust which represent numerically and economically dominant communities of the state have had to face serious financial difficulties in raising adequate funds once they began an endeavour of establishing colleges in quick succession.[4] The most poignant example is provided by the unique experience of the Nair Service Society which towards the end of the 1940s undertook the stupendous task of starting simultaneously three colleges, one at Trivandrum, another at Changanacherry and a third at Pandalam. It was only the unquestioned leadership, indomitable courage and firm determination of the legendary Mannath Padmanabhan under whose initiative and tender care the Nair Service Society was born and nurtured, that made the fund-raising campaign successful.[5] Confronted with major obstacles in raising funds, the NSS invented a new technique of financing known as *Ulpanna Pirivu* (produce collection) according to which each household was to donate in cash a certain percentage of whatever agricultural produce it raised. This remarkably ingenious technique fetched about Rs. 6.5 lakhs.

For colleges started by other organisations, particularly the christian churches, the problem of raising funds varied from management to management. While relatively rich (mostly Catholic) dioceses like those of Trichur, Palai and Changanacherry found it possible to finance the founding of colleges largely out of own resources, the task was not so smooth in respect of colleges started by other dioceses, especially the non-Catholic churches. In the case of colleges run by individual parishes of the christian churches the problem was of a different order and magnitude. Since most such parishes derived stable and substantial incomes through the offeratory received in the church especially during the annual "perunal" (religious festivals), they were in a position to raise adequate funds from own resources. The St. Aloysius College run by the St. George Church, Edathua, St. Mary's College run by the St. Mary's Jacobite Church, Manarcad, and St. George College owned by St. George Church, Aruvithura, are typical examples of such colleges. There is a close parallel between these colleges and the Guruvayurappan College, Calicut (under the management of the local Hindu community), which received in 1952 a handsome grant of Rs. 5 lakhs from the surplus funds of the Guruvayurappan temple at Guruvayur. However, even in such cases (of relatively rich dioceses and parishes) own resources are supplemented by donations. The pattern of fund-raising, as noted elsewhere, followed by the different agencies is seen to be in general, similar.

Subsequent Capital Expenditures and Recurring Expenditures

Once affiliation is granted by the University to a college for certain courses of study, the institution officially comes into existence. Any expansion of the college in terms of admission of additional batches of students for the courses already in existence or starting of additional courses (at the undergraduate,

graduate or postgraduate levels) would necessitate raising of funds to build additional classrooms and to provide additional laboratory and library facilities. In recent years the University Grants Commission has been extending financial assistance to private colleges for meeting in full or in part items of expenditure such as purchase of books and journals for the library, construction of hostels for students, etc. The majority of colleges in Kerala, however, have not been taking full advantage of the UGC assistance owing partly to lack of initiative and partly to unfamiliarity with the rules and procedures.

Among items of capital expenditures indispensable to the growth of any college, mention may be made of additional buildings to accommodate additional classes, laboratories and library. Many colleges included in our study benefited also by the munificence of individual philanthropists.[6]

Among items of recurring expenditure, the most important is 'salaries' of the teaching and nonteaching staff. Since the implementation of the 'Direct Payment Agreement' of 1972 between the state government and the managements of private colleges, payment of salaries has become the responsibility of the government. In return, the colleges are bound to remit the tuition fees collected into the government treasury. Under this agreement other recurring expenditures such as maintenance of buildings are also met by the government. The Direct Payment Agreement was the culmination of a series of attempts made to regulate and standardise the financial management of colleges about which there had existed long-drawn criticism from teachers, educationalists and the general public.

In the preceding paragraphs we briefly indicated how in Kerala the enormous cost of establishing colleges was met mostly from private sources. We shall now refer to the phases through which private colleges in Kerala have passed in relation to their finances. Mainly three periods are discernible, namely (1) the period prior to 1962, (2) the period from 1962 to 1972, and (3) the period since 1972.

I. *Period Prior to 1962*

The period prior to 1962 began with the establishment of the first college in Kerala in the early nineteenth century. It represents a period of almost complete financial autonomy for private colleges. The only control was the academic control exercised by the university in matters such as courses and syllabi, norms of admission of students to different courses and qualifications for appointment of lecturers and professors. The government almost entirely kept aloof from the functioning of private colleges. The fees collected from students were retained by the colleges concerned and were used for payment of salaries of teachers and other staff and for other expenses. There were only 36 private Arts and Science colleges in the entire State of Kerala prior to 1962. We have not been able to collect from all these colleges detailed data on rates of tuition fees and teachers' salaries which prevailed during this period. The information furnished by the Mar Ivanios College, Trivandrum, for the years 1950-51 and 1961-62 is presented in Table 3.1 to provide an indication of the order of magnitude of the rates. Only minor variations are reported to have existed in the rates among the different private colleges.

The level at which colleges operated during this period was much lower than at present mainly because of low enrolment of students. Low enrolment meant low receipts from tuition fees on the one hand and small number of teachers and hence low expenditure on salaries, on the other. The data shown in Table 3.2 pertaining to Mar Ivanios College, Trivandrum, is illustrative of the limited scale of operations of colleges of those days.

TABLE 3.1: Tuition Fees (Annual)

	1950-51 (Rs.)	1961-62 Rs.)
Intermediate	108	112 (Pre-University)
B.A.	128	140
B.Sc.	140	140
M.Com	-	200
M.Sc.	-	200
Salaries (inclusive of allowances)	Principal	450
	Professor	400
	Lecturer	220

TABLE 3.2: Level of operations of the Mar Ivanios College, Trivandrum, 1949-50 to 1958-59

Year	No. of Students	No. of teaching staff	Total fees collected (Rs.)	Salary of teaching and non-teaching staff (Rs.)
1949-50	N.A.	N.A.	23,818	12,621
1950-51	620	N.A.	92,608	45,784
1951-52	1,000	N.A.	1,44,644	76,968
1952-53	907	N.A.	1,44,400	92,666
1953-54	951	47	1,76,510	1,09,870
1954-55	1,200	51	1,96,044	1,30,305
1957-58	923	46	1,15,478	1,11,663
1958-59	1,097	56	1,41,615	1,25,210

N.A. = Not Available.

Source: Data supplied by the office of the Mar Ivanios College, Trivandrum.

The above data reveal two major features of college finances during the period prior of 1962. In the first place, the level of financial operations was low. Even as late as 1958-59, it was below Rs. 2 lakhs per annum. Secondly, while in the beginning the surplus of fees collected over expenditure on salary of staff was substantial (almost 50%), towards the end of the period under review the surplus came down drastically and became nominal. Obviously the colleges were slowly moving towards a situation of increasing difficulty to meet even their expenditure on salaries out of tuition fees. At the same time the teachers of private colleges were organising themselves along trade union lines and demanding higher salaries on a par with teachers in government colleges.

At the time of the formation of the Kerala State in November 1956 there existed different scales of pay for teachers of private colleges as between Travancore-Cochin and the Malabar region. In 1957 for the first time the government announced uniform scales of pay for teachers in private and government colleges. Lecturers were to start on a basic pay of Rs. 150. In 1958 a modified scheme of University Grants Commission (UGC) pay scales was introduced according to which the starting salary of lecturers was fixed at Rs. 200. No allowances were permissible under this scheme. Assistance from the UGC for payment of salaries to teachers in private colleges at the stipulated rates was promised only up to the end of 1961. The teachers, however, insisted that the enhanced scales of pay should continue beyond 1961 and launched an agitation for securing their demand. They argued that instead of the UGC, the state government should provide the managements of private colleges the additional funds required to pay them salaries at the existing rates. The Grant-in-Aid Code of 1962 was the direct outcome of this agitation.

II. *Period 1962-1972*

According to the Grant-in-Aid Code implemented with effect from 1st April, 1962, a sum of money was annually set apart by the state government "with the object of maintaining, improving and extending higher secular education". The grants were to be given to all affiliated private colleges subject to the conditions specified in the Code. It was made obligatory for persons or bodies sponsoring new colleges and or taking steps for affiliation of the colleges to the university to obtain the sanction of the state government in order to be eligible for grants-in-aid. The managements of private colleges which came within the purview of the grant-in-aid scheme were required to execute an agreement to abide by the terms, conditions and directions contained in the Code as well as any other directives issued by the government from time to time. Under the new Code the government was empowered to refuse grants to any institution which did not observe the principle of reservation of seats for students belonging to scheduled castes, scheduled tribes and other specific backward communities in the state.

Under the new dispensation colleges were entitled to three different types of grants-in-aid: (1) teaching grants (for salaries of teachers), (2) building grants (for the purchase, acquisition, erection or enlargement of buildings for the colleges and the hostels attached to it) and (3) equipment grants (for the purchase of books for libraries, apparatus for laboratories and furniture). All the grants were to be disbursed by the Director of Collegiate Education. No aided college, however, was allowed to spend any portion of its grant for non-educational purposes of the institution. The grant-in-aid code conferred on the government the right to refuse aid in respect of any teacher in an aided college found unfit to be a teacher.

Teaching Grant: The grant was considered supplementary to the income of the college from fees, endowments, subscriptions, donations, and other sources. During a given year the teaching grant was paid to the college on the basis of its receipts and expenditures during the previous financial year. The amount of the grant was determined in each case by the Director of Collegiate Education. The grant was, however, limited to 80 per cent of the excess of the remaining expenditure over the income from tuition fees, reckoned at standard rates, in the previous financial year. The remaining 20 per cent of the recurring expenditure was made up from the management's own funds. Approved recurring expenditure for purposes of grant-in-aid consisted of expenditure on teaching staff, nonteaching staff, taxes, ordinary repairs and upkeep, contingencies and other miscellaneous items. The government also had fixed standard rates of annual tuition fees which ranged from Rs. 104 for the pre-university/predegree course to Rs. 128 for postgraduate courses. According to the scales of pay of teaching staff fixed by the government for private colleges, the maximum pay of the principal of a college offering postgraduate courses was Rs. 1,100, that of the principal of a college having only degree courses was Rs. 1,000, the minimum pay of lecturer was Rs. 300 and that of tutor/demonstrator Rs. 175.[6] The grant-in-aid code also laid down the minimum qualification of first or second class postgraduate degree for professors and lecturers. Third class degree holders who had been granted exemption by the university prior to 1st April, 1966 were allowed to continue in their respective posts. Creation of new posts of tutors/demonstrators was to be discontinued from the time the Grant-in-Aid Code came into force. Instead, posts of junior lecturers in the scale of Rs. 175-10-275 for which the minimum qualification was the same as for lecturers were permitted to be created against vacancies of tutors/demonstrators. A minimum period of ten years' teaching experience was prescribed for promotion to or appointment as first or second grade professor in private colleges.

The pattern and number of teaching staff who came within the purview of the Grant-in-Aid Code had to conform to the norms laid down by the University regarding work load.

Nonteaching Grant: The grant-in-aid scheme also covered the nonteaching staff of colleges provided the colleges conformed to the pattern laid down by the government. Accordingly scales of pay were fixed for different nonteaching posts like clerk, accountant, typist, librarian, mechanic, laboratory attender, gasman etc. The permissible number of each post was to be fixed in relation to the number of students. For colleges with a strength of 500 or below a total of 10 nonteaching staff was permitted (clerk, accountant, cashier etc.: 3; librarian: 1; library attender: 1; and peons, watchmen, sweepers, gardeners etc.: 5). One additional post in the categories of clerk, accountant, etc., and peon watchman, etc., were allowed for every 150 students in excess of 500. The number of laboratory attenders was fixed in relation to the science subjects and courses concerned.

With the implementation of the Grant-in-Aid Code which came into force on 1st April 1962, private colleges entered a new phase as far as their finances were concerned. Earlier there had not existed a uniform pattern of financing and, as we have seen, the salaries of the teaching and nonteaching staff were paid entirely out of the tuition fees collected (except for a short period when the colleges received a grant from the UGC for payment of salaries of teachers at rates stipulated by it). Consequently, salaries used to be in general much lower than those in government colleges. Further, the annual expenditure on the salaries of the teaching and nonteaching staff of the private colleges had been lower than the amount raised by way of tuition fees. This relationship was reversed with the introduction of the Grant-in-Aid Code. From then on the expenditure on the salaries of the teaching and nonteaching staff far exceeded the tuition fees collected, as shown in Table 3.3.

TABLE 3.3: Finances of Private Colleges after the Introduction of the Grant-in-Aid Code: The Case of Selected Colleges, 1965-66 to 1970-71

(Rs.)

	1965-66		1966-67		1967-68		1968-69		1969-70		1970-71	
	Fees collected	Salaries paid	Fees collected	Salaries paid	Fees collected	Salaries paid	Fees collected	Salaries paid	Fees collected	Salaries paid	Fees collected	Salaries paid
1. Christian College, Kattakada	37808	28838	76534	91966	74001	118055	137638	155560	73429	165553	106869	179452
2. NSS College Manjeri	26792	26153	77129	84657	96713	84835	76993	104828	71043	107696	106906	116191
3. Payyannur College, Payyannur	44408	39151	89544	114583	89336	155279	NA	NA	122863	208659	126700	283951
4. St. Paul's College, Kalamasserry	23904	27553	59936	54140	88978	88501	97427	105655	95847	112655	105426	123606

Source: Data collected from the colleges. NA = Not available.

In most cases, the annual expenditure on salaries (of teaching and nonteaching staff) far exceeded receipts from tuition fees after the introduction of the Grant-in-Aid Code. The Code thus considerably eased the finances of the private colleges. In the process, however, it increased the financial dependence of the colleges on the government. On the other hand, the Code was a major gain for the college teachers since for the first time parity was established between teachers in private and government colleges in respect of salaries and grades.

III. *Period Since 1972*

The Grant-in-Aid Code did not, however, resolve the longstanding conflict between the managements and the teachers. The latter accused the former of several malpractices. A major source of conflict was insecurity of tenure. The teachers contended that unless the government assumed the responsibility of paying them directly, their rights would not become justiciable. They also demanded retirement benefits such as pension and gratuity on a par with those in government service. Further they insisted on promotion for lecturers to the next grade (which later came to be designated as noncadre second grade professorship) on the basis of a minimum prescribed period of eligible service. And finally the teachers demanded unification of fees in private colleges as well as unification of fees as between the private and the government colleges. At the end of an agitation which lasted three months from June to August 1972, the "Direct Payment Agreement" was reached between the state government, the managements and the teachers' organisations.

According to the terms and conditions of the Agreement, all educational agencies should collect tuition fees and fines only at the rates prescribed by the University from time to time (it should be noted that the university does not enjoy absolute powers in prescribing fees as it needs the concurrence of the government). The tuition fees thus collected should be remitted to the credit of the government in the treasury in the head of account suggested for the purpose. Besides tuition fees, the educational agency is also empowered to collect from the students special fees as may be prescribed by the University. Special fees thus collected should be remitted in the treasury in the name of the principal and could be withdrawn only for incurring expenditures for purposes for which such fees were collected. No fees other than those prescribed under the Agreement were to be collected from students.

Under the 'Direct Payment Agreement' all appointments to the teaching staff of the college are to be made from a panel of names prepared by "The Committee for selection of Teaching Staff" provided for in the Agreement. The committee consists of two representatives of the Educational Agency, one member nominated by the Educational Agency from among the principals, heads of departments or professors in the college/colleges with the concurrence of the University, one member chosen by the Educational Agency from among the Secretaries to Government and/or district collectors and one subject expert to be chosen by the Educational Agency from a panel of names consisting of not less than five members prepared by the University. A representative of the Educational Agency serves as the chairman of the selection committee. The Educational Agency has the option to have all the members of the teaching staff selected purely on merit from candidates of all communities or to reserve every alternate vacancy or 50 per cent of the total number of vacancies for being filled on the basis of merit from among the candidates belonging to the community of the Educational Agency. In practice, however, it has been alleged that appointments to the teaching posts in many private colleges are not made purely on merit and that donations are insisted on as a precondition for appointment. We shall be discussing this problem in greater detail later.

Just as in the case of appointments to teaching posts, members of the nonteaching staff also have to be, under the Direct Payment Agreement, selected by a 'Committee for selection of nonteaching staff'. The committee consists of two representatives of the Educational Agency and one member chosen by the Educational Agency from the Officers of the government of the cadre of Revenue Divisional Officer or Deputy Collector.

The Direct Payment Agreement also laid down norms for admission of students to the institutions concerned. Accordingly 20 per cent of the total number of seats in each college under the Educational Agency should be reserved for students belonging to scheduled castes and scheduled tribes. If all the 20 per cent seats thus reserved cannot be filled by SC/ST students, the unfilled seats are to be filled on the basis of merit from among the backward minority communities in case the college is run by a backward minority community and from among the other backward communities in all other cases. Ten per cent of the seats in colleges run by forward communities and 20 per cent run by backward communities are reserved for the students of the community to which the college concerned belongs. However, these seats have to be filled strictly on the basis of merit from among the students of that community. Fifty per cent of the seats in forward community colleges and 40 per cent in backward community colleges are to be filled by the Educational Agency on the basis of open merit. The remaining 20 per cent of the seats constitutes the management quota which may be allotted at the discretion of the management – a practice which, as we shall see later, has led to much abuse.

Financial Provisions of the Direct Payment Agreement

(1) Payment of Pay and Allowances of Teaching and Nonteaching Staff

From 1st September, 1972, the government assumed direct responsibility to disburse, through the principal of the institution concerned, salaries to the teaching and nonteaching staff. The government was not liable for any claims of the teaching and nonteaching staff towards their pay and allowances or provident fund or gratuity or any other payment relating to any period prior to September 1972 except and to the extent provided in the Agreement. The pay and allowances paid to the teaching and nonteaching staff for the month of March 1972 were adopted as the pay and allowances of the respective members for the period from September 1972. The payment of grant-in-aid that had been in force till that date under the Grant-in-Aid Code from 1962 and all other payments were discontinued with effect from 1st June, 1972. From then on the Educational Agency was entitled to receive only those payments provided for in the Direct Payment Agreement. It was liable to refund to the government any excess payment it had received towards grant-in-aid for any of the provisions when such excess was detected after the audit of accounts for the periods concerned.

(2) Contingency Grant

According to the Direct Payment Agreement, the Government has undertaken to pay the Educational Agency a grant towards contingency expenditure for each academic year. The grant for each college is calculated on a per capita basis for each category of students by levels – Predegree, Degree and Postgraduate – and by subjects – Arts and Sciences.

Of this grant 50 per cent has to be paid in advance in April or May and the rest before the end of the year.

(3) Maintenance Grant

The government has also agreed to pay the Educational Agency every academic year a grant towards maintenance and repairs of the college, calculated on a per capita basis with the help of the Public Works Department of the government. A separate ceiling is worked out for Arts and Science sections and Predegree, Degree and Postgraduate classes. Fifty per cent of this item of grant is to be paid in advance in April or May and the rest before the end of the year.

(4) Library and Laboratory Grant

Further, the government pays a grant towards library and laboratory on the basis of the norms worked out in consultation with the University.

The Direct Payment Agreement was the final act in a series of measures adopted to redress the longstanding grievances of teachers regarding scales of pay, security of service and retirement benefits. In all these respects parity was established between teachers in private and government colleges. However, the managements retained the right to make appointments although the teachers had wanted all appointments to be made through the Public Service Commission. In financial terms the Direct Payment Agreement has imposed a heavy burden on the government. In addition to meeting the expenditures on account of different grants to the colleges outlined above, the government has had to incur also additional administrative costs to set up several offices of deputy directors of collegiate education to disburse the grants as well as for other administrative purposes.

NOTES

1. The only published works available which throw some light on the problems of financing colleges relate to the colleges run by the Nair Service Society. These works consists of (1) *History of the Nair Service Society* (Malayalam), N.S.S. Press, Changanacherry, 1971, (2) *Golden Jubillee Commemoration Volume of the Nair Service Society* (Malayalam), India Press, Kottayam 1964, and *Complete works of Mannam* (Malayalam) Chief Editor: Kidangoor A.N. Gopalakrishna Pillai (Vidhyarthi Mitram Press, Kottayam, 1978).
2. In granting affiliation to new colleges, universities have definite rules regarding the extent of land to be made available in rural and urban centres. According to the existing rules, the educational agency should be in possession of 12 acres of land in rural areas and 7 acres in urban areas in respect of Arts and Science colleges.
3. See K.V. Eapen, *Church Missionary Society and Education in Kerala* (Kollet Publications, Kottayam, 1985) p. 124 and V. Nagam Aiya, *The Travancore State Manual Vol. II* (Government Press, Trivandrum 1906) p. 47.
4. Today both organisations run a chain of Arts and Science colleges spread all over the state. The Nair Service Society and the Sree Narayana Trust have under their corporate management 14 Arts and Science colleges each.
5. The campaign was started at Quilon in 1947 by accepting donations of Rs. 10,000 each from three prominent citizens, one of whom was Narayana Swami Reddiar who did not belong to the Nair Community. For a vivid account of the fund-raising campaign, see the article "Half a century of Nair Service Society" (Malayalam) by P.K. Parameswaran Nair in the *Golden Jubilee Volume of Nair Service Society* (India Press, Kottayam, 1964).
6. To mention only a few instances: soon after the opening of the Payyannur College in July 1965, a building to provide accommodation for the teaching and nonteaching staff, was donated by Dr. K.P. Meenakshi Amma in memory of her late husband. The Shanmukha Mudaliyar hostel of the Guruvayurappan College was the result of a donation from V. Nataraja Mudaliar and P.S. Nair of the Calicut Tile Company. The construction of a library hall of the Mahatma Gandhi College, Trivandrum, was made possible by the donation of Rs. 50,000 by Smt. Lakshmi Pillai Kochamma.
7. The scales of pay fixed were as follows:
   (a) Principal of colleges having postgraduate courses -

Rs. 800-50-1100

(b) Principal of colleges having only degree courses - Rs. 700-50-1000

(c) Professor Grade I of postgraduate departments - Rs. 700-50-1000

(d) Principal of Junior colleges without degree courses - Rs. 400-30-640-40-800

(e) Professor Grade II of departments offering only degree courses - Rs. 400-30-640-40-800

(f) Lecturer - Rs. 300-20-400-25-600

(g) Tutor/Demonstrator - Rs. 175-10-275.

4

PATTERN AND TRENDS OF FINANCING OF COLLEGES IN THE PRIVATE SECTOR: Institutional Sources

As we have noted in the previous chapter, with the introduction of 'direct payment', the state government assumed responsibility for the payment of: (1) salaries of the teaching and nonteaching staff, (2) library and laboratory grant, (3) maintenance grant, and (4) contingency grant, of private colleges in the state. These items together account for the major part of the recurring expenditure of a college. Thus the state government is now playing an undoubtedly predominant role in the financing of colleges in the private sector. The other institutional sources of finance, though far less important, consist of the management (the educational agency), the universities to which the colleges are affiliated, and the University Grants Commission. In the following sections we discuss the different sources of institutional finance available to private colleges and the changes that have taken place in its pattern in the recent past. The discussion is based on the data collected from a sample of 25 colleges which, as pointed out in the introductory chapter, represents a cross-section of private colleges in the state in terms of region and type and community of management. The data relate to the period since 1972, the year in which the system of 'direct payment' was introduced. As already mentioned, private colleges are seen to have been unsystematic and negligent in maintaining records, especially proper accounts. It was only after the direct intervention of the government in 1972 that colleges became compelled to keep proper records on a regular basis. Yet the accounts being maintained by several colleges have not improved much. It becomes particularly difficult when one tries to compile financial data on a time-series basis. Consequently, there do exist several gaps in the data on receipts and expenditures we have collected, especially those relating to the earlier years. Despite this obvious limitation, the available data do provide valuable insights into the functioning of private colleges. Since several agencies are involved in the financing of colleges, we may first discuss the relative role played by each. In Table 4.1 we present the broad pattern of institutional financing of colleges in the private sector since 1972.

The data clearly show that the total financial assistance received by colleges have been rapidly on the increase and that the relative importance of each institutional agency of financing has undergone significant change. For instance, the total assistance per college which was only Rs. 2.42 lakhs in 1972-73, rose to a hefty Rs. 29.27 lakhs in 1985-86, registering an eleven-fold increase. The phenomenal increase in the funding of colleges is a reflection of not only rapidly rising costs of running colleges but also the expansion of the colleges in terms of enrolment of students, levels of education and number of courses offered at each level. While on the one hand the pay scales of the teaching and nonteaching staff have been going up with the implementation of the recommendations of successive State Pay Commissions, on the other hand the number of staff members itself has been increasing with the upgradation of colleges from junior to degree and from degree to postgraduate.

TABLE 4.1: Institutional Financing of Selected Private Colleges in Kerala (Average Amount Per College), 1972-73 to 1985-86

(Rs.)

Source	1972-73	1973-74	1974-75	1975-76	1976-77	1977-78	1978-79
1	2	3	4	5	6	7	8
1. State Government	222810(91.97)	373292(95.07)	519576(96.78)	711460(95.52)	8713113(96.33)	990432(94.37)	1212908(93.21)
2. Management	6112(2.52)	8003(2.04)	4961(0.92)	6231(0.84)	16210(1.79)	12507(1.19)	8607(0.66)
3. U.G.C.	11375(4.70)	8500(2.16)	8788(1.64)	17245(2.31)	9511(1.05)	33893(3.23)	63038(4.84)
4. University	430(0.18)	1515(0.38)	1921(0.36)	4021(0.54)	4293(0.48)	5366(0.51)	5272(0.41)
5. Others*	1534(0.63)	1360(0.35)	1627(0.30)	5904(0.79)	3171(0.35)	7295(0.70)	11502(0.88)
Total	242261(100)	392670(100)	536873(100)	744861(100)	904498(100)	104498(100)	1301327(100)

(Contd.)

TABLE 4.1 — *Contd.*

Source	1979-80	1980-81	1981-82	1982-83	1983-84	1984-85	1985-86
1	9	10	11	12	13	14	15
1. State Government	1176142(93.65)	1398389(95.91)	1623559(94.42)	1972239(95.95)	2153962(94.93)	2460431(92.94)	2697806(92.17)
2. Management	11550(0.92)	17537(1.20)	62653(3.64)	14035(0.68)	16268(0.72)	73434(2.77)	40786(1.39)
3. U.G.C.	54908(4.37)	30634(2.10)	15138(0.88)	44900(2.18)	68857(3.03)	74235(2.81)	158843(5.43)
4. University	5700(0.46)	6323(0.43)	11230(0.66)	7439(0.36)	9929(0.44)	10601(0.40)	12322(0.42)
5. Others*	7563(0.60)	5216(0.36)	6905(0.40)	16968(0.83)	19989(0.88)	28602(1.08)	17390(0.59)
Total	1255863(100)	1458099(100)	1719485(100)	2055581(100)	2269005(100)	2647303(100)	2927147(100)

* Others consist of NCC Directorate, Sports Council, Planning Commission, All-India Research Organisations like ICSSR, CSIR, ICAR, etc.

Note: Figures in parentheses refer to percentages.

The state government is the major institutional agency for the financing of private colleges. Government grants per college increased from Rs.2.23 lakhs in 1972-73 to Rs.26.98 lakhs in 1985-86. The proportion of financial support by the state government has consistently remained at more than 90 per cent of the total. In fact its share varied from 91.97 per cent (in 1972-73) to 96.78 per cent (in 1974-75). Among the other agencies, the University Grants Commission and the College Management are the important ones. While the average financial assistance from the University Grants Commission increased from Rs.11,375 in 1972-73 to Rs.1.59 lakhs in 1985-86, the corresponding increase in the funds provided by the Management has been from Rs.6,112 to Rs.40,786. In contrast to the grants from the state government, the financial assistance by these two agencies varied considerably from year to year. In relative terms the assistance varied from 0.66 per cent in 1978-79 to 3.64 per cent in 1981-82 in the case of the management and from 0.88 per cent in 1981-82 to 5.43 per cent in 1985-86 in respect of the U.G.C. Such variations are due to the differences in the types of institutional funding. Financial assistance from the University to which the college is affiliated has remained meagre, well below 1 per cent (below 0.15 per cent for most years). The university's relationship with the affiliated colleges consists mainly in guidance and control of their academic programmes.

A more detailed source-wise analysis of financial assistance is attempted below:

1. Grants from the State Government

In Table 4.2 we present a break-up of government grants received since 1972-73.

Among the grants received from the state government, those for salaries (of teaching and

TABLE 4.2: Average State Government Grants to Sample Colleges, 1972-73 to 1985-86

(Rs.)

Purpose of grant	1972-73	1973-74	1974-75	1975-76	1976-77	1977-78	1978-79
1	2	3	4	5	6	7	8
1. Salaries of teaching and nonteaching staff	215905(96.90)	355286(95.18)	504278(97.06)	689885(96.97)	847280(97.24)	961031(97.03)	1186159(97.80)
2. Library			374(0.07)	1713(0.24)	232(0.03)	956(0.10)	750(0.06)
3. Laboratory	164(0.08)	132(0.03)	462(0.09)	1431(0.20)	251(0.03)	1005(0.10)	787(0.07)
4. Maintenance	716(0.32)	1309(0.35)	959(0.18)	2266(0.32)	2296(0.26)	3638(0.37)	4885(0.40)
5. Scholarships and Stipends	5821(2.61)	12173(3.26)	12036(2.32)	15141(2.13)	18677(2.11)	20228(2.04)	18370(1.51)
6. Contingency	204(0.09)	4392(1.18)	1467(0.28)	1024(0.14)	2877(0.33)	3574(0.36)	1957(0.16)
Total	222810(100)	373292(100)	5195576(100)	711460(100)	871313(100)	990432(100)	1212908(100)

(Contd.)

TABLE 4.2 — *Contd.*

Purpose of grant	1979-80	1980-81	1981-82	1982-83	1983-84	1984-85	1985-86
1	9	10	11	12	13	14	15
1. Salaries of teaching and nonteaching staff	1147872(97.60)	1365956(97.68)	1591226(98.01)	1913326(97.01)	2090302(97.04)	2405672(97.78)	2647334(98.13)
2. Library	169(0.01)	446(0.03)	555(0.03)	1190(0.06)	787(0.04)	693(0.03)	292(0.01)
3. Laboratory	745(0.06)	1175(0.09)	2054(0.13)	3401(0.17)	2554(0.12)	587(0.02)	1600(0.06)
4. Maintenance	1769(0.15)	1604(0.11)	1377(0.09)	2457(0.13)	660(0.13)	5(0.00)	6307(0.23)
5. Scholarships and Stipends	2564(2.15)	29062(2.08)	27322(1.68)	49858(2.53)	58365(2.71)	52140(2.12)	41235(1.53)
6. Contingency	323(0.03)	146(0.01)	1025(0.06)	2007(0.10)	1294(0.06)	1334(0.06)	1038(0.04)
Total	1176142(100)	1398389(100)	1623559(100)	1972239(100)	2153962(100)	2460431(100)	2697806(100)

Note: Figures in parentheses refer to percentages.

nonteaching staff) are by far the most important. For our sample of 25 colleges, the average grant for salaries per college increased from Rs.2.16 lakhs in 1972-73 to Rs.26.47 lakhs in 1985-86, the latest year for which we have data. The steady growth of grant under this head is explained by two factors. First, with a steady increase in enrolment and opening of additional courses at different levels – predegree, degree and postgraduate – the number of teachers, and to some extent of nonteaching staff, also goes up.[1]

Second, with the establishment of parity between the pay scales of the teachers and the nonteaching staff of the government and private colleges, the wage bill on this account has been steadily on the increase. The 'Direct Payment Agreement' entered into by the state government with the management and the teachers' organisations of private colleges has thus proved to be a heavy financial burden to it. It may, however, be added that though the grant per college towards salaries has increased several times, its relative share in total government grants has remained more or less unchanged, varying within a narrow range, from 95.2 per cent in 1973-74 to 98.1 per cent in 1985-86. The variations observed are due largely to delays in payments and the consequent accumulation of arrears which are disbursed during the subsequent year or years. Such delays are common in respect of other government grants (library, laboratory, etc.) also.

Next to grants for payment of salaries of teaching and nonteaching staff come scholarships and stipends. During the period prior to the 'Kumara Pillai Commission' Report (1966) the state government had provided scholarships and stipends only to students belonging to the scheduled castes and scheduled tribes. With the implementation of the Kumara Pillai Commission Report (KPCR) and the subsequent liberalisation of its provisions, students belonging to other communities – forward as well as backward – with parental incomes not exceeding a certain prescribed limit, also became eligible to receive scholarships and stipends from the state government. (The present annual income limit for eligibility to scholarships and stipends under KPCR is Rs.20,000). In addition to full fee concession, such students are also entitled to an annual lump sum grant and a monthly stipend, the amount of the stipend depending upon whether the students are day scholars or hostelers. Students belonging to the scheduled castes and scheduled tribes receive monthly stipends at higher rates.

The average grant per college for scholarships and stipends increased from Rs. 5,821 in 1972-73 to Rs. 41,235 in 1985-86. During the same period its share in total grants declined from 2.6 per cent to 1.5 per cent.

These two items of grants (salaries of teaching and nonteaching staff, and scholarships and stipends) together account for over 99 per cent of the government grant. The remaining four types of grant – library, laboratory, maintenance and contingency – therefore constitute less than one per cent of the total.

Payment of salaries of the staff, and scholarships and stipends offered to the students are in a sense committed expenditures of the government. There can be no going back on them. Teachers of private colleges consist of large numbers (each college having 100-150 teachers); besides they are a highly unionised and articulate group. Considerable political clout is wielded by office bearers of teachers' organisations each of which owes allegiance to one political party or another. Some of such teachers also hold office in political parties. Naturally the government cannot afford any lapse in the payment of their salaries. Welfare of Harijans and other economically and socially backward communities and groups is a politically sensitive issue. Therefore, the government pays adequate attention to this aspect also by adopting a fairly liberal scheme of scholarships and stipends. However, when it comes to items of expenditure as, for example, those on libraries and laboratories, which directly contribute to the academic performance of the college, the pressure groups do not back them up and naturally the government grants for such purposes are reduced to absolutely meagre amounts. This fact is evident from the data presented in Table 4.2. But why is it that pressures similar to the ones in respect of payment of salaries of teachers and scholarships and stipends of students have not developed with regard to other items of grants? Why is it that the students and even the teachers themselves have not resented the inadequacy of resources for libraries and laboratories? Broadly speaking, this is explained by the lack of motivation and commitment on the part of the teachers and the students alike. We have already referred to the total unionisation of the college teachers and their serious involvement in political activity. It should not be surprising that in such an environment professionalism becomes an early casualty. Add to these negative factors the various malpractices associated with the appointment of teachers. The emerging scenario is a very depressing one. The lack of motivation on the part of the majority of the students is mostly rooted in the stagnation of the state economy. A major proportion of the students enrolled in Arts and Science colleges have found their way to these institutions because they have nothing else to do. With the mounting unemployment in the state, students are compelled to seek admission to colleges as a temporary relief measure. No wonder the bulk of the student community is least bothered by the inadequacy of the library and laboratory facilities. The average amount per sample college has varied from Rs.169 in 1979-80 to Rs.1,713 in 1975-76 in the case of library grants and from Rs. 132 in

1973-74 to Rs. 3,401 in 1982-83 in respect of laboratory grants. For the entire 14-year period under review, the average annual government grant per sample college for library came to a mere Rs.534 and that for laboratory only Rs. 1,168, their combined share in total government grants remaining less than 0.5 per cent. Reckoned in terms of the current costs of books and periodicals and laboratory equipment and chemicals, it is obvious that the amounts allotted are deplorably inadequate. Such meagre allotments are indicative of the relatively low priority which considerations of quality of higher education have received in the state. Of course, as mentioned above, one should not lose sight of the fact that for quality of education the commitment of the teachers, whose salary is fully met by the government, is equally, if not more, important. The limitation is partially overcome by the managements of some colleges by supplementing the library and laboratory grants received from the government with allotments out of their own funds. However, all managements are not equally resourceful or enlightened in this respect. Besides these two sources, the University Grants Commission has also begun extending substantial assistance to colleges (known as Basic Assistance to Arts, Science, Commerce and Multi-faculty colleges for books and journals and equipment) for the development of their library and laboratory facilities since the beginning of the Sixth Five Year Plan period. The fact remains, however, that the majority of the colleges in Kerala have not taken advantage of the UGC assistance.

In respect of maintenance grant also the situation remains unsatisfactory. For the sample colleges, the average annual maintenance grant increased from Rs. 716 in 1972-73 to Rs. 6,307 in 1985-86, the average for the entire 14-year period being Rs. 2,161. Maintenance of buildings is nowadays very expensive. Since most colleges have large buildings, the amounts annually released by the government for maintenance are found to be quite insufficient. In this connection we may note that under the Direct Payment Agreement the government follows certain norms for fixing the grant to be paid to each college in a year for different purposes: library, laboratory, contingency and maintenance. In practice, however, even the grants allotted (inadequate as they may be) are not released in time owing to several technical reasons such as delays in the completion of audit of accounts relating to the previous years. Several principals of colleges have complained about such delays. For instance, the S.D. College, Alleppey, has yet to receive contingency grant from the government from 1977-78 onwards accounting for a total sum of Rs.3.36 lakhs till 1986-87. For the same period a total sum of Rs.86,835 is due to this college from the government towards maintenance grant. Because of the poor maintenance many college buildings are in a rundown condition. With leaky roofs and disfigured walls, they present an altogether inelegant and uncongenial atmosphere for academic pursuits.

Net Grant from the Government

As the tuition fees collected by the colleges are remitted into the government treasury, the gross amount disbursed by the government by way of grants does not constitute the actual burden to the government. The burden is represented by the difference between total grants and total receipts from tuition fees. Since complete data on tuition fees are not available for all the sample colleges and for all the years, in Table 4.3 we present the average annual government grant, annual tuition fees and the average net government grant per college for eleven of the sample colleges[2] for the period 1976-77 to 1985-86.

TABLE 4.3: Net Grant received from the State Government, 1976-77 to 1985-86: Selected Colleges

(Rs. lakhs)

	1976-77	1977-78	1978-79	1979-80	1980-81	1981-82	1982-83	1983-84	1984-85	1985-86
1	2	3	4	5	6	7	8	9	10	11
1. Total grant	11.42	11.59	13.86	12.32	14.82	18.39	21.28	21.13	25.53	27.78
2. Tuition fees	2.04	2.04	2.30	2.69	2.51	2.99	3.46	3.26	2.96	3.67
3. Net grant	9.38	9.55	11.56	9.63	12.31	15.40	17.82	17.87	22.57	24.11
4. Percentage of 2 to 1	17.84	17.60	16.60	21.82	16.93	16.29	16.24	15.41	11.61	13.21

It is seen that tuition fees collected from students have formed less than 18 per cent of the grant provided by the government throughout the period except in 1979-80 when it amounted to 21.8 per cent. While government grant per college increased from Rs.11.42 lakhs in 1976-77 to Rs.27.78 lakhs in 1985-86 registering a more than 143 per cent increase, tuition fees increased from Rs.2.04 lakhs to Rs.3.67 lakhs registering a less than 80 per cent increase. The increase observed in the amount of tuition fees collected is obviously due to increase in enrolment and not due to increase in the rates. In fact, the rates of tuition fees now in force in Kerala are one of the lowest in the whole country. The prevailing rates are given below:

Course	*Tuition fees (annual) (Rs)*
Predegree	124
B.A./B.Com./B.Sc.	144
M.A./M.Sc/M.Com.	160

Since the tuition fees as well as other fees are fixed by the government and not by the universities, a uniform set of rates prevails in all the three affiliating universities of Kerala, namely Kerala, Mahatma Gandhi and Calicut. Besides tuition fees, several minor fees are collected such as admission, library, magazine, sports, laboratory, etc., which are earmarked for specific expenditures within the colleges concerned and are, therefore, not remitted into the government treasury.

It has been pointed out that the tuition fees prevailing in Kerala have no relation to either the expenditure incurred by the government for running the colleges or the ability-to-pay of the guardians of vast sections of the student community. As the high level committee on education and employment (appointed by the State Planning Board) rightly points out in its Report on Higher Education, "It is paradoxical that students are so much accustomed to nominal fees in colleges that they have a tendency to protest against the increase in fees in the colleges, while they are prepared to shell out heavy fees in tutorial institutes or parallel colleges".[3] It may be mentioned that in several universities in the neighbouring States of Tamil Nadu and Karnataka, the tuition fees in force for different courses are much higher. For instance, while the annual fees for the B.A./B.Sc. course in these universities vary from Rs.240 to Rs.300, they are only about half these amounts in Kerala (see Appendix VII of the Report on Higher Education referred to). Obviously one way to strengthen the finances of private colleges as well as government colleges is to raise the tuition fees to reasonable levels and at the same time to provide full fee concession to all those who deserve it.

2. Grants from the Management (Educational Agency)

In the establishment and the subsequent running of colleges there always has existed a sort of partnership between the government and the educational agency concerned. The Grant-in-Aid Code of 1962 and later the Direct Payment Agreement of 1972 recognised this partnership. While the state government shoulders the major responsibility in financing the recurring expenditures of the private colleges, wherever government grants fall short of the requirement, the managements concerned make attempts to supplement them. However, such supplementary financing is normally possible only for managements which have independent resources as, for instance, in the case of large corporate managements like the Sree Narayana Trust, the Nair Service Society and the Muslim Educational Society.

The financial support mobilised by the

management from own resources, from time to time, to supplement the current receipts of the college may itself comprise donations received by the management from teachers, students and/or parents and members of the general public. Whether the entire amount thus collected goes into financing of college expenditure is not clear. The fact remains, however, that the managements seldom maintain accounts of expenditures, thus incurred, in the registers of the colleges concerned. On a perusal of the accounts we notice that the funds thus raised are in most instances not recorded as current receipts in the college accounts; instead, they are shown as receipts from donations in the managements' accounts which are not subject to the scrutiny of government audit. We have earlier noted that during 1972-73 to 1985-86 receipts from the management increased from Rs. 6,112 to Rs. 40,786 and that their percentage in total institutional finance declined from 2.5 per cent to 1.4 per cent. We shall not briefly discuss the composition of expenditure met out of the contributions made by the management (Table 4.4).

It is seen that over the years the financial assistance per college received from the management has, in absolute terms, increased considerably from Rs. 6,112 in 1972-73 to Rs. 40,786 in 1985-86. The trend has been thus a rising one. However, no consistent pattern is in evidence due to the fact that the management normally steps in only to supplement the funds available from other sources in times of need. When a college is hardpressed for funds and no resources are in sight, it approaches the management for help. If funds were available from other sources, the management would be reluctant to spend out of its own resources. It is, therefore, in respect of such expenditures as are not financed by other agencies that the management assumes the responsibility. Land and buildings are generally treated as the

TABLE 4.4: Average Financial Assistance Per Sample College received from the Management, 1972-73 to 1985-86

(Rs.)

Purpose of assistance	1972-73	1973-74	1974-75	1975-76	1976-77	1977-78	1978-79
1	2	3	4	5	6	7	8
1. Land and buildings	3712.8(60.74)	7186(89.79)	264(5.32)	809(12.98)	8795(54.26)	3876.4(30.99)	4342(50.45)
2. Maintenance	208.3(3.41)	—	1226(24.71)	1036(16.63)	221(1.36)	—	1642(19.08)
3. Library (books & periodicals)	318.9(5.22)	250(3.12)	—	1941(31.15)	628(3.88)	1084.3(8.67)	283(3.29)
4. Laboratory (equipment & chemicals)	544.8(8.91)	264(3.30)	157(3.17)	968(15.54)	5408(33.36)	4370.4(34.95)	899(10.44)
5. Furniture	999.7(16.36)	—	729(14.69)	896(14.38)	629(3.38)	718.8(5.75)	17(0.20)
6. Others*	327.7(5.36)	303(3.79)	2585(52.11)	581(9.32)	529(3.26)	2456.7(19.64)	1424(16.54)
Total	6112.2(100)	8003(100)	4961(100)	6231(100)	16210(100)	12506.6(100)	8607(100)

(Contd.)

TABLE 4.4 — *Contd.*

Purpose of assistance	1979-80	1980-81	1981-82	1982-83	1983-84	1984-85	1985-86
1	9	10	11	12	13	14	15
1. Land and buildings	632(5.47)	1192(6.80)	51620(82.39)	2314(16.49)	908(5.58)	54599.8(74.35)	9238(22.65)
2. Maintenance	2836(24.56)	1215(6.93)	1906(3.04)	3245(23.12)	3543(21.78)	1374.2(1.87)	13210(32.39)
3. Library (books & periodicals)	1469(12.71)	6321(36.04)	2280(3.74)	890(6.34)	1393(8.56)	1311.4(1.79)	1614(3.96)
4. Laboratory (equipment & chemicals)	4296(37.20)	3463(19.74)	1658(2.65)	2466(17.57)	7204(44.28)	12249.0(16.68)	5764(14.13)
5. Furniture	635(5.50)	2646(15.09)	3006(4.80)	1210(8.62)	2165(13.31)	3419.2(4.66)	10104(24.77)
6. Others*	1682(14.56)	2700(15.40)	2183(3.48)	3910(27.86)	1055(6.49)	480.0(0.65)	856(2.10)
Total	11550(100)	17537(100)	6253(100)	14035(100)	16268(100)	73433.6(100)	40786(100)

* Others include conduct of seminars, conferences, etc.

Note: Figures within perentheses refer to percentages.

responsibility of the management. This is borne out by our data. During the period 1972-73 to 1985-86 relatively large amounts were provided by the managements for purchase of land and construction of buildings. In certain years the average amount per sample college rose to Rs.50,000 or even more. In terms of its relative share also, land and buildings occupy a pre-eminent position. Next to land and buildings, financial support for laboratories was also a major item of support by managements. As with land and buildings, setting up laboratories for the different courses in science subjects also involves considerable initial investment. Of course, according to the provisions of the Direct Payment Agreement, colleges are entitled to laboratory grant from the government based on certain norms. In practice, however, the grants have proved to be nominal. Furthermore, they are not released on a regular basis because of procedural delays. For instance, the S.D. College, Alleppey, was entitled to a laboratory grant of Rs.19,865 in 1981-82. Since this amount was not released by the Department of Collegiate Education, the College was prevented from claiming the laboratory grant for the subsequent years. It is precisely because of the inadequacy of the laboratory grant under the Direct Payment Agreement that managements are compelled to step in with own additional funds in support. This is true of library grants also. Financial support of the management for the development of the college library is, however, of a much smaller magnitude as is evident from Table 4.4.

3. Grants from the University Grants Commission

Though the management is supposed to have a direct stake in the development of the college it has taken the initiative to establish, it is the University Grants Commission which has been extending sizeable financial assistance to colleges in the private sector, second only to the State government. In fact the role of the UGC has been steadily expanding in recent years. "Basic Assistance to Colleges" consisting of faculty improvement programmes, books and journals, and essential laboratory equipment – a scheme initiated during the Sixth Five Year Plan Period – has continued under the Seventh Plan also. Under the Faculty Improvement Programme, up to a maximum of 5 teachers (depending on the number of permanent teachers in the college) could be deputed to undergo the M.Phil. course during the VII Plan Period. The teachers thus deputed receive a monthly stipend of Rs. 500 in addition to their normal salary. The UGC also meets the cost of appointing a substitute in the place of the teacher deputed for the course. Besides, the UGC also provides assistance for the development of undergraduate and postgraduate education to those colleges which fulfil certain eligibility conditions stipulated by it. Under the programme of development of undergraduate education the University Grants Commission provides assistance not only for purchase of books, journals and equipment but also for construction of buildings for academic uses including extension of library and laboratory, hostels for students and teachers, staff quarters, canteen building, health centre etc. The extent of assistance varies from 50 per cent to 100 per cent of the actual cost subject to a prescribed ceiling. However, it is seen that several colleges do not avail themselves of the UGC assistance due partly to lack of information regarding the rules and the procedures and partly to lack of initiative. With the formation of College Development Councils in most universities and the appointment of a senior officer as Director of such Councils, the situation is expected to improve. Details of UGC assistance received by our sample colleges since 1972-73 are presented in Table 4.5.

TABLE 4.5: Average Financial Assistance Per Sample College Received from the University Grants Commission, 1972-73 to 1985-86

(Rs.)

Purpose	1972-73	1973-74	1974-75	1975-76	1976-77	1977-78	1978-79
1	2	3	4	5	6	6	7
1. Buildings	3961(34.82)	1913(22.50)	2300(26.17)	12251(71.04)	1354(14.24)	13985(41.26)	20022(31.76)
2. Books and journals	2771(24.36)	2849(33.52)	3135(35.67)	4153(24.08)	4128(43.40)	6072(17.91)	17441(27.67)
3. Laboratory equipment	1539(13.53)	1389(16.34)	2636(30.00)	208(1.21)	3968(41.72)	2090(6.17)	11067(17.56)
4. Faculty improvement	208(1.83)	17(00.20)	336(3.82)	165(0.96)	—	671(1.198)	2479(3.93)
5. Others*	2896(25.46)	2332(27.44)	381(4.34)	468(2.71)	61(00.64)	11075(32.68)	12029(19.08)
Total	11375(100)	8500(100)	8788(100)	17245(100)	9511(100)	33893(100)	63038(100)

(Contd.)

TABLE 4.5 – *Contd.*

Purpose	1979-80	1980-81	1981-82	1982-83	1983-84	1984-85	1985-86
1	9	10	11	12	13	14	15
1. Buildings	25217(45.93)	14120(46.09)	1223(8.08)	14675(32.68)	18912(27.46)	23799(32.06)	56423(35.52)
2. Books and journals	13795(25.12)	9106(29.72)	3443(22.74)	11788(26.26)	14728(21.39)	13475(18.15)	40971(25.79)
3. Laboratory equipment	13632(24.83)	6120(19.98)	2043(13.50)	12457(27.74)	20786(30.19)	19992(26.93)	19571(12.32)
4. Faculty improvement	1910(3.48)	1026(3.35)	8229(54.36)	5027(11.20)	7711(11.20)	10727(14.45)	35734(22.50)
5. Others*	354(0.64)	262(0.86)	200(1.32)	953(2.12)	6720(9.76)	6242(8.41)	6144(3.87)
Total	54908(100)	30634(100)	15138(100)	44900(100)	68857(100)	74235(100)	158843(100)

* 'Others' refer to assistance for physical education programmes, national adult education programme, etc.

Note: Figures within parentheses refer to percentages.

The grants from the University Grants Commission have registered a significant increase; the average amount per sample college increased from Rs. 11,375 in 1972-73 to Rs. 1,58,843 in 1985-86. Notwithstanding the year-to-year variations in the quantum of assistance, the trend has been definitely upward. In this connection it should be borne in mind that these figures are averages arrived at by including also those sample colleges which did not avail themselves of any financial assistance at all from the UGC. The average amount per college which actually availed of UGC grants, has been impressive.

Among the various purposes for which assistance of the University Grants Commission was received, buildings are the most important. As we have already noted, the UGC has a fairly liberal scheme of assistance for construction of academic buildings such as library and laboratory buildings, students' and teachers' hostels, staff quarters etc. During the 14-year period under review, UGC assistance for buildings increased from Rs. 3,961 in 1972-73 to Rs. 56,423 in 1985-86; during the same period the percentage share of buildings increased from 34.8 per cent to 35.5 per cent. However, considerable variations are noted from year to year in the average amount per sample college as well as in its relative share in total assistance. While the average amount varied from Rs. 1,223 in 1981-82 to Rs. 56,423 in 1985-86, the relative share varied from 8.08 per cent in 1981-82 to 71.04 per cent in 1975-76. Among individual colleges which made substantial use of UGC assistance for buildings, mention may be made of Mar Ivanios College, Trivandrum (Rs.5.56 lakhs during 1978-81), Catholicate college, Pathanamthitta (Rs.8.16 lakhs during 1979-86), Sir Syed College, Taliparamba (Rs. 9 lakhs during 1975-86), S.N. College, Quilon (Rs.3.69 lakhs in 1985-86), Guruvayurappan College, Calicut (Rs.2.56 lakhs in 1982-83) and Mar Thoma College, Tiruvalla

(Rs.2.83 lakhs during 1977-81).

Next in importance is the assistance given for books and journals. While the average amount of assistance per college for the purchase of books and journals increased from Rs. 2,771 in 1972-73 to Rs. 40,971 in 1985-86, its relative share increased only marginally from 24.4 per cent to 25.8 per cent. As in the case of UGC assistance for buildings, the average assistance per college for books and journals also has varied considerably from year to year from Rs. 2,771 in 1972-73 to Rs. 40,971 in 1985-86, the relative share having varied from 17.9 per cent in 1977-78 to 43.4 per cent in 1976-77. Generally speaking grants for buildings, and books and journals account for the major share of UGC assistance to colleges. All the remaining items together usually account for only about 4 per cent of the assistance.

4. Financial Assistance from the University

Financial support from the University, along with the assistance from the UGC, may be treated as a source of public funding for private colleges since the University derives the bulk of its grants directly from the government. However, the University to which the college is affiliated plays only a negligible role in its financing. Under the affiliating system, the university's role in relation to affiliated colleges is chiefly one of academic leadership and guidance, say, of prescribing syllabi and curricula for the various courses and of conducting examinations. As regards financial relationship, there is only a very limited flow of funds taking place from the university to the colleges which consist of (1) University merit scholarships and (2) Grants for National Service Scheme. Details of assistance received by the sample colleges from the university for the period under review are furnished in Table 4.6.

Except during 1973-74 and 1974-75, assistance

from the University for National Service Scheme has surpassed the provision for merit scholarships. There is obviously a strong case for increasing the number and amount of merit scholarship awarded by the University. This is, however, linked up with the broader question of the University's resources. Since the University itself is largely dependent on the state government for funding, there are powerful financial constraints on what it can do for affiliated colleges.

5. Other Sources of Institutional Finance

In addition to the sources of finance outlined in the preceding paragraphs, colleges in the private sector receive varying amounts of grants from the N.C.C. Directorate (for expenses connected with the functioning of the unit of the National Cadet Core in the college), the Sports Council and all-India research organisations like the ICSSR, ICAR, CSIR, etc. These grants are earmarked for specific purposes and consist of very limited amounts. Except for the NCC, units of which function in most colleges, grants from research organisations are not taken advantage of by most of the colleges since they do not have many research guides with the required qualifications on the staff.

In the foregoing chapter we have discussed in some detail the various sources of institutional finance available to colleges in the private sector in Kerala. Notwithstanding the possible gaps in the data, the major finding that has emerged from our analysis is that colleges are heavily dependent on the state government for financial support. This, in turn, is the inevitable outcome of the responsibility the state government has assumed for the payment of the entire salary of the teaching and nonteaching staff. Apart from meeting this obligation, precious little is done either by the state government or the Universities to improve higher education in the

TABLE 4.6: Average Financial Assistance Per Sample College Received from the University, 1972-73 to 1985-86

(Rs.)

Purpose	1972-73	1973-74	1974-75	1975-76	1976-77	1977-78	1978-79
1	2	3	4	5	6	7	8
1. Merit scholarships	212(49.30)	1429(94.32)	1272(66.22)	1378(34.27)	1297(30.21)	1757(32.69)	1588(30.12)
2. National Service Scheme	218(50.70)	86(5.68)	649(33.78)	2643(65.73)	2996(69.79)	3612(67.31)	3684(69.88)
Total	430(100)	1515(100)	1921(100)	4021(100)	4293(100)	5366(100)	5272(100)

TABLE 4.6 — *Continued*

Purpose	1979-80	1980-81	1981-82	1982-83	1983-84	1984-85	1985-86
1	9	10	11	12	13	14	15
1. Merit scholarships	1790(31.40)	1115(17.63)	537(4.79)	744(10.00)	487(4.90)	889(8.39)	744(6.04)
2. National Service Scheme	3910(58.60)	5208(82.37)	10693(95.21)	6695(90.00)	9442(95.10)	9712(9.61)	11578(93.96)
Total	5700(100)	6323(100)	11230(100)	7439(100)	9929(100)	10601(100)	12322(100)

Note: Figures within parentheses refer to percentage.

state. Aid from the University Grants Commission which could go a long way in filling this gap is taken advantage of by only a handful of colleges which are more resourceful and have superior leadership.

NOTES

1. The process of expansion of staff is seen to have followed a typical pattern: at the first stage of the starting of a new college, government sanction is restricted to a limited number of batches of the Predegree classes. Soon pressure is exerted on the government and the University to sanction additional batches for the predegree course. After some more time the management approaches the authorities for upgradation of the college to the degree level. In such efforts the management naturally attempts to strengthen its claim by seeking the support of a few influential politicians also. Once the college gets up graded to degree level, further efforts are unleashed to get sanction for the starting of postgraduate courses. Thus what is begun as a modest junior college ends up within a few years as a postgraduate institution, regardless of whether such an institution is required on the basis of considerations of economic efficiency or educational priorities.
2. The 11 colleges for which data are available are: (1) Christian college, Kattakada, (2) NSS College, Nilamel, (3) St. Aloysius College, Edathua, (4) Mar Thoma College, Tiruvalla, (5) FMN College, Quilon, (6) NSS College, Manjeri, (7) SN College, Quilon, (8) SN College, Chelannur (9) Payyannur College, (10) Bishop Moore College, Mavelikara, and (11) Devaswom Board College, Sasthamcotta.
3. High Level Committee on Education and Employment, State Planning Board: Report on Higher Education (Trivandrum: 1984) p.14.

5

PATTERN AND TRENDS OF FINANCING OF COLLEGES IN THE PRIVATE SECTOR: Non-institutional Sources

We had a fairly long discussion in the previous chapter on the institutional sources of financing of private colleges. As we have noted, institutional sources involving mainly four agencies, namely the state government, the management (i.e. the educational agency) the University Grants Commission and the University to which the college is affiliated, together account for a substantial share of the total receipts of the colleges. In 1985-86, the latest year for which data have been presented, the average annual amount received per private college in Kerala came to Rs. 29.27 lakhs. If allowance is made for the possible underreporting or gaps in information supplied by the colleges, the actual amount must be still higher. About 92 per cent of the institutional finance received by the colleges in 1985-86 came from the state government. In the present chapter we focus our attention on non-institutional sources of financing. They consist mainly of: (1) fees other than tuition fees, (2) donations, and (3) miscellaneous receipts such as income from property, interest on bank deposits and borrowings. As we have noted in Chapter 3, according to the terms and conditions of the Direct

Payment Agreement, colleges are empowered to collect certain items of fees including tuition fees - but only at stipulated rates. However, the colleges are required to remit the entire tuition fees collected into the government treasury in view of the fact that the government is directly responsible for the payment of the salary of both the teaching and the nonteaching staff. Since we have treated the payment of the salary of the teaching and nonteaching staff as receipts of the college from the state government, we do not treat tuition fees collected and remitted into the government treasury as a receipt item in order to avoid double counting. All the other items of fees collected are retained by the college and the principal is competent to spend the amounts for stipulated purposes. They include application fee, admission fee, library fee, laboratory fee, games fee, magazine and calendar fee, college union fee, caution deposit, association fees, medical examination fee etc. As far as these fees are concerned, the rates are fixed by the government from time to time and the total collection per college would depend directly on enrolment. Hence there is little likelihood of underreporting of such receipts. This cannot, however, be said of donations. It is most likely that there is considerable underreporting of donations because of the controversial nature of this item. The colleges are required to keep accounts of only those amounts of donations which are received in the college office. Donations collected by the management may not be reflected fully in the accounts of the colleges. It is well known that several college managements in Kerala insist on payment of donations for appointment of teachers and admission of students under "the management quota". Such donations are in general retained by the managements themselves and not released to the colleges under the head 'donations'. The amounts shown in the accounts of a college as 'receipts from the management' in a particular year are likely to be only a fraction of what the management actually received by way of 'donations'. If, on the other hand, the donations of a given year are passed on to the college during a subsequent year, the total amount could as well exceed the donations of that year. The real question is whether, over a period of time, the donations collected are spent in full on the development of the concerned college or not. A related, but more general, question is whether the practice of collecting donations is justified at all and if so, to what extent, for what purpose and under what conditions. We shall be discussing these issues presently. The donations included in Table 5.1 refer to amounts received directly in the college office. Since these amounts are entered in the accounts of the college under the head 'receipts', obviously the college has had no intention to suppress the source. In other words, what is documented below is the official record of the donations collected by the sample colleges.

Receipts per sample college from non-institutional sources increased from Rs. 89,019 in 1972-73 to Rs. 2,26,799 in 1985-86. Of course much variation is seen to have taken place from year to year in the receipts from this source. It varied from Rs. 61,775 in 1973-74 to Rs. 3,01,119 in 1984-85. Of the three types of non-institutional finance, fees (excluding tuition fees) have accounted for the bulk of the receipts throughout the period under review, their relative share varying from 51.4 per cent in 1972-73 to 84-5 per cent in 1975-76.

1. Fees (other than tuition fees)

As we have already noted, various fees which are earmarked for specific purposes are levied from students. Most of such fees are collected at the time of admission and retained by the college in the form of a bank deposit in the name of the principal to be used as and when the need arises. The entire

TABLE 5.1: Average Receipts Per Sample College from Non-institutional Sources (1972-73 to 1985-86)

(*Rs.*)

Source	1972-73	1973-74	1974-75	1975-76	1976-77	1977-78	1978-79	1979-80
1	2	3	4	5	6	7	8	9
1. Fees	45750(51.4)	43664(70.7)	58830(84.3)	72095(84.5)	85907(79.9)	89579(74.9)	1020811(77.3)	127716(76.0)
2. Donations	5308(6.0)	2958(4.8)	3571(5.1)	4826(5.6)	5488(5.1)	2628(2.2)	5147(3.3)	26967(16.1)
3. Others (miscellaneous)	37961(42.6)	15153(24.5)	7368(10.6)	8443(9.9)	16164(15.0)	27371(22.9)	30365(19.4)	13282(7.9)
Total	89019(100)	61775(100)	69769(100)	85364(100)	107559(100)	119578(100)	156323(100)	167965(100)

TABLE 5.1 — *Contd.*

Source	1980-81	1981-82	1982-83	1983-84	1984-85	1985-86
1	10	11	12	13	14	15
1. Fees	121905(59.0)	150126(70.4)	175205(68.8)	170647(69.6)	186583(62.0)	177146(78.1)
2. Donations	33113(16.0)	40871(19.1)	43082(16.9)	58972(24.1)	91338(30.3)	31679(14.0)
3. Others (miscellaneous)	51744(25.0)	22329(10.5)	36286(14.3)	15431(6.3)	23198(7.7)	17974(7.9)
Total	206762(100)	213326(100)	254573(100)	245050(100)	301119(100)	226799(100)

Note: Figures within parentheses refer to percentages.

caution deposit (library and laboratory) however, is returned to the students at the time of their completing the course or leaving the institution, after making adjustments for damages or losses caused, if any. Since these fees are fixed in amount and cannot be diverted for other purposes, the colleges have no reason to conceal their source or to manipulate the accounts. However, it has not been possible to obtain full data on fees collected since many colleges do not have complete records especially for earlier years. In spite of the gaps in the data, it is seen that fees fetch substantial revenue to the colleges. The average receipts per college from this source increased from Rs. 45,750 in 1972-73 to Rs. 1,77,146 in 1985-86. Since fees are levied on a per capita basis, any increase in enrolment of students is followed by a corresponding increase in the amount of fees collected. The average amounts of the different types of fees (other than tuition fees) collected per college during 1972-73 and 1985-86 are presented in Table 5.2.

Among the various fees, five items, namely caution deposit, games fee, laboratory fee, admission fee, and magazine and calendar fees form the most important ones and together account for over 50 per cent of the total amount collected. Further, substantial increase is observed in the miscellaneous item 'other fees' from 13.18 per cent in 1972-73 to 20.52 per cent in the 1985-86.

2. Donations

Donations received by the colleges may be classified into (a) donations from staff - teaching and nonteaching, (b) donations from students and/or parents and (c) donations from the general public. Since the amounts collected under these items are shown in the accounts of the colleges concerned, we may presume that they were collected for legitimate purposes with the tacit permission of the government. However, there is also a distinct possibility that donations are insisted on as a precondition for appointments or admissions and that such payments are recorded as voluntary donations for worthwhile and unobjectionable causes such as the addition of a college building, auditorium, library building, stadium, gymnasium etc. This could be the nature also of donations received directly by the managements. A detailed break up of the different sources of donations as recorded in the college accounts is shown in Table 5.3.

TABLE 5.2: Average Amount of Fees (Other Than Tuition Fees) Collected Per Sample College, 1972-73 and 1985-86

(Rs.)

Types of fees	1972-73	1985-86
1. Application fee	2537.96(5.55)	6841.36(3.86)
2. Admission fee	4909.52(10.73)	16266.88(9.18)
3. Library fee	2463.92(5.39)	8946.12(5.05)
4. Laboratory fee	4233.63(9.25)	19413.72(10.96)
5. Games fee	6947.88(15.19)	21642.(12.22)
6. Magazine & Calendar fee	3266.21(7.14)	15198.60(8.58)
7. College Union fee	966.92(2.18)	4577.12(2.58)
8. Caution deposit	11065.58(24.19)	36107.72(20.38)
9. Association fee	1597.54(3.49)	6736.36(3.80)
10. Medical examination fee	1369.83(2.99)	3238.16(1.83)
11. Audio-visual fee	331.13(0.72)	1824.04(1.03)
12. Other fees	6029.58(13.18)	36353.16(20.52)
Total	45749.70(100.00)	177145.54(100.00)

Note: Figures within brackets refer to percentages.

It is seen from Table 5.3 that donations from the staff appear the least significant of all the sources. While the average amount per sample college has varied from Rs. 511 in 1975-76 to Rs. 3,340 in 1981-82, in most years such donations formed less

TABLE 5.3: Average Receipts of Sample Colleges from Donations, 1972-73 to 1985-86

(Rs.)

Source	1972-73	1973-74	1974-75	1975-76	1976-77	1977-78	1978-79	1979-80
1	2	3	4	5	6	7	8	9
1. Staff	1127(21.23)	1241(41.95)	569(15.93)	511(10.59)	1097(19.99)	1072(40.79)	1203(23.37)	1518(5.63)
2. Students and/or Parents	3795(71.50)	1131(38.24)	1559(43.66)	525(10.88)	895(16.31)	1321(50.27)	1799(34.95)	2015(7.47)
3. General Public	386(7.27)	586(19.81)	1443(40.41)	3790(78.53)	3496(63.70)	235(8.94)	2145(41.68)	23434(86.90)
Total	5308(100)	2958(100)	3571(100)	4826(100)	5488(100)	2628(100)	5147(100)	26967(100)

TABLE 5.3 — *Contd.*

Source	1980-81	1981-82	1982-83	1983-84	1984-85	1985-86
1	10	11	12	13	14	15
1. Staff	1388(4.19)	3340(8.17)	1393(3.25)	2630(4.46)	1783(1.95)	1579(4.98)
2. Students and/or Parents	2100(6.34)	20882(51.09)	18604(43.18)	21085(35.75)	19843(21.72)	18146(57.28)
3. General Public	29625(89.47)	16649(40.74)	23080(53.57)	35257(59.79)	69712(76.33)	11954(37.74)
Total	33113(100)	40871(100)	43082(100)	58972(100)	91338(100)	31679(100)

Note: Figures within parentheses refer to percentages.

than one-fifth of the total amount of donations; in several years they amounted to less than one-tenth. It should, however, be emphasised that out of the sample of 25 colleges selected for the study, data on donations from the staff were furnished only by five colleges. Among these five, the St. Aloysius, Edathua, had data only for one year (1981-82). If we confine our analysis to the remaining four colleges for which data on donations from staff are available for a number of years, the resulting picture is very different from what is indicated in Table 5.3. The relevant data are presented in Table 5.4. Of the four colleges listed, Guruvayurappan College shows a record of consistently fairly high donations from the staff.

It is well known that 'donations' from students and/or parents and the general public have remained much more important, than is indicated by the Tables 5.3 and 5.4, as a source of finance for managements of private colleges. The figures shown in these two tables do not indicate any consistent trend; if in certain years donations from students and/or parents out weighted those from the general public, at other times the situation was the reverse. While the average donation per college from students and/or parents has varied from Rs. 525 in 1975-76 to Rs. 21,085 in 1983-84, its relative share has fluctuated between 8.3 per cent in 1980-81 and 71.5 per cent in 1972-73. The corresponding figures for donations from the public were Rs. 235 in 1977-78 and Rs. 69,712 in 1984-85, and 7.3 per cent in 1972-73 and 89.5 per cent in 1980-81. The limitation of data arising from the low percentage of colleges reporting donations referred to earlier applies equally to donations from students and/or parents, and the general public. Only seven colleges reported donations from students and/or parents, and six colleges from the general public for varying periods from one to fourteen years. S.D. College (Alleppey), Guruvayurappan College (Calicut) and

TABLE 5.4: Donations from Staff: Reporting Colleges only, 1972-73 to 1985-86

(Rs.)

Reporting colleges	1972-73	1973-74	1974-75	1975-76	1976-77	1977-78	1978-79
1. N.S.S College, Nilamel	—	—	—	—	—	3166	4822
2. M.E.S College, Ponnani	258	277	441	754	586	420	181
3. Guruvayurappan College, Calicut	20250	24000	13200	11500	9685	8000	7400
4. Nirmalagiri College, Koothuparamba	6550	5500	—	—	16050	14130	16460
Total	27058	29777	13641	12254	26321	25716	28863
Average per college	6764.50	7444.25	3410.25	3063.50	6580.25	6429	7215.75

TABLE 5.4: *Contd.*

Reporting collages	1979-80	1980-81	1981-82	1982-83	1983-84	1984-85	1985-86
1. N.S.S College, Nilamel	7699	4235	7824	6812	20020	10848	—
2. M.E.S College, Ponnani	440	763	1770	2600	2875	2135	1925
3. Guruvayurappan College, Calicut	13250	20075	14850	5200	15510	15850	17550
4. Nirmalagiri College, Koothuparamba	15035	8240	14560	20330	27350	15750	20000
Total	36424	33313	39004	34942	65755	44583	39475
Average per college	9106	8328.25	9751	8735.50	16438.75	11145.75	9868.75

Bishop Moore College (Mavelikara) have reported substantial donations in certain years from students and/or parents. For instance, during the 5-year period from 1981-82 to 1985-86, S.D. College collected on an average Rs. 4.54 lakhs yearly. During the same period the average amount received by the Guruvayurappan College came to Rs. 27,810 per annum. During the period 1972-73 to 1975-76 the Bishop Moore College raised on an average Rs. 29,800 annually from donations from students and/or parents. As regards donations from the general public, three colleges namely M.S.M. College (Kayamkulam), Guruvayurappan College (Calicut), and Payyannur College (Payyannur) have reported substantial amounts by way of donations. During the 6-year period from 1979-80 to 1984-85, the M.S.M. College received on an average Rs. 4.60 lakhs per year as donations from the public. The record of Guruvayurappan college has been less impressive; during the 13-year period from 1973-74 to 1985-86 it raised an average annual donation of Rs. 17,901 only. It is highly doubtful that all these donations were in the nature of voluntary payments made for the good of the college concerned. At least in the case of a few institutions which are known to collect compulsory donations for appointments and admissions, there is a distinct possibility that amounts thus realised are not entered at all in the accounts of the college; in cases in which they are, the entry would be as 'voluntary' contributions. For instance, it is reliably learnt that compulsory donations collected for appointment to teaching and nonteaching posts by Payyannur College were entered as voluntary donations 'from the general public' in the accounts of the college.

3. Miscellaneous Receipts

In addition to donations some colleges also derive varying amounts of receipts from a few

TABLE 5.5: Average Receipts Per Samples College from Miscellaneous Sources, 1972-73 to 1985-86

(Rs.)

Source	1972-73	1973-74	1974-75	1975-76	1976-77	1977-78	1978-79	1979-80
1	2	3	4	5	6	7	8	
1. Income from property	120(0.32)	107(0.71)	200(2.71)	143(1.69)	133(0.82)	162(0.59)	262(0.86)	
2. Interest on bank deposits	442(1.16)	153(1.01)	767(10.41)	1219(14.44)	774(4.79)	535(1.96)	813(2.68)	
3. Borrowings	37399(98.52)	14893(98.28)	6402(86.88)	7082(83.87)	15257(94.39)	26673(97.45)	29290(96.46)	
Total	37961(100)	15153(100)	7369(100)	8444(100)	16164(100)	27370(100)	30365(100)	

TABLE 5.5 — *Contd.*

Source	1979-80	1980-81	1981-82	1982-83	1983-84	1984-85	1985-86
1	9	10	11	12	13	14	15
1. Income from property	279(2.10)	735(1.46)	635(2.84)	1439(3.97)	1480(9.59)	1477(6.37)	1557(8.66)
2. Interest on bank deposits	845(6.36)	1728(3.34)	2320(10.39)	4598(12.67)	2997(19.42)	4201(18.11)	2336(13.00)
3. Borrowings	12158(91.54)	49263(95.00)	19375(86.77)	30249(83.36)	10954(70.99)	17520(75.52)	14081(78.34)
Total	13282(100)	51744(100)	22330(100)	36286(100)	15431(100)	23198(100)	17974(100)

Note: Figures within parentheses refer to percentages.

miscellaneous items such as income from property, interest on bank deposits, borrowings from different sources, etc. (Table 5.5).

Among the miscellaneous sources 'borrowings' is the most prominent. When a college finds that its current receipts are inadequate, it might resort to borrowing. In most cases, it is the Principal, on authorisation by the Governing Council of the college, who arranges the loan (in colleges under individual management, the Principal is often the secretary of the Governing Council). While borrowings have naturally varied from year to year, over the years their importance has declined in absolute as well as relative terms. From Rs. 37,399 in 1972-73, average borrowing per sample college declined to Rs. 14,081 in 1985-86; in relative terms the decline has been from 98.5 per cent to 78.3 per cent of the total miscellaneous receipts. The highest borrowing of Rs. 49,263 per sample college was recorded in 1980-81 and the lowest of Rs. 6,402 in 1974-75. Apparently with the attainment of greater stability in other sources of receipts borrowings have become relatively less important. On the other hand, considerable improvement is seen to have taken place in the income from property and interest on bank deposits. The increase in income from bank deposits has been particularly impressive. The average amount per sample college under this head increased from Rs. 442 in 1972-73 to Rs. 2,336 in 1985-86.

The Financing of Colleges: The Increasing Role of Donations

We have earlier noted that most private colleges receive substantial amounts as donations from students and/or parents, teachers and members of the general public. Donations may be received by either the college or the management. While the donations recieved directly in the college office are entered in the accounts of the college, amounts received by the management (educational agency) are included in the accounts of the educational agency. Since the college accounts are subject to government audit, it is very likely that normally the major share of the donations are received by the management and shown as such in its accounts. So long as the management spends these donations for the development of the college, such a procedure does not seem to matter. It is, however, quite possible that at least some managements divert a portion — in all probability a major portion — of the donations thus raised to purposes totally unrelated to the development of the college. Under such circumstances the running of a college becomes a business proposition. Apart from the routing of the donations, which by itself should not raise any serious issues, there is the question of deliberately suppressing the purpose for which donations are received. Donations received for appointment of teachers and admission of students are shown as donations from the general public for unobjectionable (and legitimate) causes such as construction of additional buildings, development of library, construction of stadia or auditoria, etc. In most instances, managements do not issue receipts for such donations. Our enquiry has convinced us that the amounts which appear in the account books of the colleges divulge only a small portion of the total funds raised by the management by way of donations.

A more in-depth probing into this issue seemed to us of great importance. The following discussion on donations is based on personal interviews and direct enquiries with teachers, students and other knowledgeable persons. While it throws further light on the financing of colleges, the discussion as such should be viewed separately from the analysis made earlier on the basis of data collected from the colleges and offices of the Department of Collegiate

Education of the State Government. The information furnished, of course, applies to the sample colleges only.

(1) *Donations for Teachers' Appointments*: It has been found that out of the sample of 25 colleges selected for the study, all except 8 colleges insist on compulsory donations as a precondition for appointment of teachers. Donations for appointments to nonteaching posts also may be prevalent in these colleges, but because of the limited size of the nonteaching staff and its close links with the principal and the management, information about this category was hard to come by. The colleges which do not receive donations for appointment to teaching posts are : (1) Mar Ivanios College, Trivandrum; (2) Mar Thoma College, Tiruvalla; (3) F.M.N. College, Quilon; (4) St. Paul's College, Kalamasserry; (5) St. Thomas College, Trichur; (6) Nirmalagiri College, Koothuparamba; (7) Bishop Moore College, Mavelikara; and (8) St. Michael's College, Shertallai. Among the colleges which at present collect donations for appointments there are a few relatively old institutions like Guruvayurappan College, Calicut; S.D. College, Alleppey; M.G. College, Trivandrum; and S.N. College, Quilon. These colleges had not insisted on donations during the initial phase of their existence. Broadly speaking, these institutions started receiving donations for appointments only after 1965. On the other hand, there are other colleges as, for example, M.E.S. College, Ponnani and St Mary's College, Manarcad, which have insisted on donations from their very inception. In several cases it has not been possible, for obvious reasons, to ascertain the year from which the practice of collecting donations began. Large numbers of teachers who entered service after paying a compulsory 'donation' would have retired by now; of those who still remain in service, many naturally declined to divulge details of the donations they

paid. In terms of the amounts of donations collected currently, the sample colleges which follow the practice - 17 in all - may be classified into three categories on the basis of the size of the donations, namely low, medium and high.

TABLE 5.6: Classification of Colleges According to Size of Donations for Appointment of Teachers

Group	Range of donations	Name of college
1. Low	Rs. 25,000 - Rs. 40,000	1. M.G. College, Trivandrum
		2. Christian College, Kattakada
		3. N.S.S. College, Nilamel
		4. N.S.S. College, Manjeri
		5. Sir Syed College, Taliparamba
		6. Guruvayurappan College, Calicut
		7. M.E.S. College, Ponnani
2. Medium	Rs. 40,000 - Rs. 55,000	1. T.K.M.M. College, Nangiarkulangara
		2. Catholicate College, Pathanamthitta
		3. S.D. College, Alleppey
		4. S.N. College, Quilon
		5. S.N. College, Chelannur
3. High	Rs. 55,000 - Rs. 75,000	1. St. Aloysius College, Edathua
		2. St. Mary's College, Manarcaud
		3. Payyannur College, Payyannur
		4. D.B. College, Sasthamcotta
		5. M.S.M. College, Kayamkulam

The above is only a rough and ready classification since there is often a good deal of secrecy about the donations. Further, we have received conflicting reports on donations from several colleges. However, it can be said that in respect of colleges run by most corporate managements like the N.S.S., the S.N. Trust, the M.E.S and the M.O.S.C. (Malankara Orthodox Syrian Church), there is relatively greater openness and more uniformity in the amount of donations collected. On the other hand, donations are generally high in respect of colleges run by individual (single) managements represented by local committees or parishes of christian churches. It is also noteworthy that the amount of the donations varies with the discipline. In those disciplines in which for every vacancy of a junior lecturer's post there are scores of applicants, the amount of donation demanded shoots high (the market mechanism of supply and demand operates brazenly here!). Interestingly, donations are collected not only from candidates for selection from the management quota of 50 per cent of the total number of appointments. Candidates who are selected on open-merit basis are also subjected to the tyranny of 'donations'. However, in fairness, it must be pointed out that in certain deserving cases (poor economic status or brilliant academic record) some managements adopt a lenient attitude by either reducing the amounts of the donations or even granting total exemption. For instance, it is learnt that for appointments under 'open-merit quota' in the colleges under the S.N. Trust no donation is insisted on if the applicant is a first – or second – rank holder in the subject. Some colleges such as the Catholicate College, Pathanamthitta, allow a concession to candidates belonging to the community which runs the college.

Wherever donations are insisted on for appointments, their full (final) incidence often exceeds the payment made to the management as payment of varying amounts has to be made also to several intermediaries including local or talk branches of the organisation running the college. Such payments may vary from Rs. 5,000 to Rs. 10,000 as in the case of N.S.S. Colleges.

As indicated earlier, information on donations for appointments to the nonteaching staff was hard to collect. However, we found that two colleges, namely Devaswom Board College, Sasthamcotta and Payyanur College, had been collecting donations (up to Rs. 30,000 in Devaswom Board College and Rs. 15,000 to Rs. 25,00 in Payyannur College) for such appointments.

Besides receiving donations at the time of the first appointment, the managements of some colleges also pressurise teachers to make liberal contributions on special occasions such as promotions. Donations are made by teachers even to protect themselves from inconvenient transfers. Other contributions normally made include those towards construction of additional college buildings, auditoria, stadia, etc. Celebration of jubilees is one of the common occasions when the staff are made to contribute at rates fixed by the management. Such donations are fairly high, often amounting to a month's salary (e.g. M.G. College, Trivandrum and Catholicate College, Pathanamthitta).

2. *Donations for Admissions*: Managements of colleges are also known to collect donations from applicants for admissions to different courses in the college under the 'management quota' which forms 20 per cent of the total seats. Such donations vary in amount with the level of the course (predegree, degree or postgraduate) and the subject/discipline. (arts, science, humanities, commerce, etc).

Out of the sample of 25 colleges, as many as 15 colleges collect donations from applicants for admissions. The colleges which do not indulge in this practice are: (1) Christian College, Kattakada, (2) Mar Ivanios College, Trivandrum, (3) Mar Thoma College, Tiruvalla, (4) F.M.N. College, Quilon, (5) St. Paul's College, Kalamasserry, (6) St. Thomas College, Trichur, (7) Nirmalagiri College, Koothuparamba, (8) Bishop Moore College, Mavelikara, (9) St. Michael's College, Shertallai, and (10) M.E.S. College, Ponnani.

Generally speaking colleges which collect donations for appointments also insist on donations for admissions. According to the information we have been able to gather, the only exceptions in this regard are Christian College, Kattakada (which accepts relatively low donations for appointments but none for admission) and M.E.S. College, Ponnani.

For the predegree course donation per student varies from less than Rs. 300 to Rs. 1,500. In general, there is a gradation of the donations on the basis of the group (of optional subjects) applied for. Science subjects attract the largest donations, commerce subjects come next and arts subjects last. While some colleges such as N.S.S. College, Manjeri, St. Aloysius College, Edathua and Payyannur college collect nominal amounts not exceeding Rs. 500 per admission to the predegree course, others such as M.S.M. College, Kayamkulam, M.G. College, Trivandrum, Catholicate College, Pathanamthitta, T.K.M.M. College, Nangiarkulangara, collect amounts in the range of Rs. 1000 - Rs. 1500, At the degree level, the average amount of donations varies from Rs. 500 to Rs. 7000, science subjects such as chemistry and physics attracting the highest amounts and humanities such as philosophy, History and Politics the lowest. While colleges such as Guruvayurappan, NSS Manjeri, Devaswom Board, and St. Aloysius charge less than Rs. 1000, others - S.D. College, T.K.M.M. College, Sir Syed College, M.S.M. College and Catholicate college - Collect much higher amounts. It is reported that M.S.M. College collects up to Rs. 7000 as capitation fee for admission to B.Sc courses. For admission to postgraduate courses, the range of capitation fee is quite wide, the amounts varying from less than 6,000 as in the case of S.D. College, Guruvayurappan College and Catholicate College to Rs. 15,000 in M.G. College and M.S.M. College.

As pointed out earlier, donations received for

appointments and capitation fees realised for admission are not recorded as such in the accounts of the colleges concerned. To the extent that such receipts are not included in the accounts of the colleges there is clearly an underreporting of receipts. If at all such receipts are accounted for, either in full or in part, they are shown as donations from teachers, parents and/or students or members of the general public for certain worthy causes and not as donations compulsorily levied for appointments or admissions. It is highly probable that for colleges run by individual (single) managements such as Payyannur College, Guruvayurappan, M.S.M., St. Aloysius, etc, compulsory donations for appointments and admissions are shown as voluntary donations from staff, parents and/or students, or the public, as the case may be, in the accounts of the college. Thus among the colleges under individual managements which are known to receive compulsory donations, it is seen that Guruvayurappan College, Calicut, collected or an average Rs. 14023 per annum between 1972-73 and 1985-86 as donations from the teaching and nonteaching staff; S.D. College, Alleppey, received on an average Rs. 4.54 lakhs yearly between 1981-82 and 1985-86 and Guruvayurappan College Rs. 2,1562 between 1972-73 and 1985-86 as donations from parents and/or students; and M.S.M. College, Kayamkulam, received on the average Rs. 4.6 lakhs yearly between 1979-80 and 1985-86, Guruvayurappan College Rs. 17,901 during the period 1973-74 to 1985-86, and Payyannur College Rs. 3.4 lakhs between 1982-83 and 1985-86 as donations from the public. For colleges run by corporate managements (e.g. N.S.S., S.N. Trust, M.E.S, etc.) such donations may not always be shown in the accounts of the colleges concerned but may be included in the accounts of the respective organisations as donations from the general public and well-wishers. In a few cases, however, the entire amounts of such donations might remain unaccounted as payments would have been made under the table.

Since the amount of donation collected per candidate is much higher for appointments compared to that for admissions, public criticism has arisen mostly against it. It is, however, important to note that while the number of permanent vacancies of teachers (as well as of nonteaching staff) arising each year may be limited (normally not more than half a dozen),* the number of students admitted under the management quota is fixed and does not vary from year to year. For those colleges which collect capitation fees, though the donation per student may be relatively small, the total amount received on this account would be quite large in view of the large numbers involved. Thus, for illustration, in a college with an annual enrolment of, say, 2500, the management quota of 20 per cent would come to 500 seats. Assuming that on the average an amount of Rs. 1000 is realised from a student as capitation fee (we may assume that the college has several degree courses as well as

* For those samples colleges affiliated to the Kerala University the maximum number of vacancies annually filled since 1983-84 are given below:

Name of College	No. of vacancies	Year/s
1. M.G. College	1	1985-86 & 1987-88
2. Mar Ivanios College	4	1983-84
3. Christian College	3	1985-86
4. N.S.S. College, Nilamel	5	1985-86
5. S.N. College, Quilon	4	1987-88
6. F.M.N. College	2	1986-87
7. M.S.M College	5	1984-85
8. Devaswom Board College	3	1983-85 & 1985-86
9. St. Michael's College	1	1984-85
10. S.D. College	4	1985-86
11. Bishop Moore College	1	1984-85, 85-86 & 1987-88

Source: Office of the Kerala University.

a few postgraduate departments), the total receipts from this source would add up to Rs. 5 lakhs. Evidently this is more than adequate to meet whatever deficiencies there might exist in the annual grants received from the state government, provided the amounts thus collected are passed on to the colleges concerned.

The practice of accepting donations for appointments and capitation fees for admissions followed by several managements of private colleges has naturally led to much criticism. On ethical grounds there is certainly no justification for the practice. Besides, standards of higher education may fall as a result of less competent teachers being appointed to the faculty and students who are otherwise ineligible for admission being enrolled. The managements' stand is that they do not particularly relish the practice of supplementing their current receipts with donations from teachers or students and that under the socio-economic conditions prevailing in Kerala they are constrained to resort to compulsory donations as an unavoidable evil. They argue that the grants received from the government, even assuming that the payment of the grants is prompt, are inadequate to meet such expenses as telephone bills, cost of electricity and water supplied to the college campus, purchase of chemicals for the laboratories, and maintenance of the college buildings. Unlike in other parts of the country, there are not many multimillionaires in Kerala who could be approached and might be willing to make large voluntary donations. Therefore the only option open to the managements, they argue, is to collect donations from the immediate beneficiaries, i.e. the staff and the students. The principal of one of the sample colleges has pointed out that if only the government permitted the colleges to collect an annual special fee of Rs. 100 or so from all the students admitted, there would arise no need for any donations, but that the government was not prepared to concede such a demand.

Apart from the questions of propriety, legality and fairness, one wonders whether the entire funds thus raised are used for meeting the needs of the college concerned. Since there is a good deal of confidentiality shrouding such donations, one does not know how much exactly is the annual receipts from this source and how much is in fact spent by the college out of such receipts. If those payments go into the funds of the management which, in turn, passes on to the college varying amounts for specific purposes, one has no means of finding out whether the donations collected are matched by an equal amount of transfer by the management over a period of time, if not during the same year of collection. Among the colleges which are known to receive donations for appointments and admissions we find that receipts from the managements as recorded in the accounts of the colleges concerned are marginal. Since complete data for all such colleges are not available, we give below (Table 5.7.) the annual average of such receipts for some colleges for the periods for which data are available.

TABLE 5.7: Receipts of Selected Sample Colleges from the Management for Selected Years

Sl. No.	Name of College	Period	No. of Years	Annual average receipts (Rs)
1.	N.S.S. College, Nilamel	1973-74 to 1982-83	10	2,9899
2.	T.K.M.M. College, Nanagiarkulangara	1978-79 to 1984-85	7	9,296
3.	M.E.S. College, Ponnani	1972-73 to 1985-86	14	37,904
4.	N.S.S. College, Manjeri	1980-81 to 1985-86	6	32,142
5.	S.N. College, Quilon	1974-75 to 1985-86	12	71,030
6.	S.N. College, Chelannur	1974-75 to 1983-84	10	13,204

Source: Data Furnished by the Colleges.

All the colleges listed belong to corporate managements such as N.S.S., S.N. Trust and M.E.S. and are known to collect donations for appointments and admissions. It is also known that these donations are routed through the management unlike in the case of individual managements. And yet the average amount spent on the colleges annually is in most cases much less than the donation reported to have been received for one single appointment of lecturer.

In the light of our discussion in the preceding paragraphs, it is clear that for those colleges/ managements which supplement their financial resources with compulsory donations received for appointments and admissions, there should be no financial problem. They might even command surplus funds. If at all they have a problem, it must be because funds thus collected are not fully channellised for the needs of the college. For those colleges which do not receive any compulsory donations (in our sample of 25 colleges, there were only 8 such colleges), there is real financial stringency. In all such cases the shortfall in funds has to be made up by voluntary gifts from members of the community owning the institution. For instance, in his monthly letter to the members of the church published in the 'Malankara Sabha Tharaka', the official organ of the Mar Thoma Syrian Church, Dr Alexander Mar Thoma Metropolitan, head of the Mar Thoma Church, while reiterating the resolve of the church not to accept any donations for appointments or admissions, had referred to the fact that the Mar Thoma College, Tiruvalla, was in debt to the tune of Rs. 7 lakhs.* In the same letter the Metropolitan appealed for gifts to free the college from the burden of debt. Of course, colleges run by relatively rich dioceses or parishes of the christian churches may be free from such financial strain.

---

* *Malankara Sabha Tharaka*, September 1988, p. 3. The debt of Rs. 7 lakhs must have been accumulated over several years.

A lasting solution to the problem of inadequate finances of colleges in the private sector could be found only if any one of the following steps are adopted:

(1) Higher grants from the state government with or without raising tuition fees.
(2) Empowering the colleges to charge the students a special fee (subject to a ceiling fixed by the government) adequate to make up the deficiency in government grants.
(3) Delinking the colleges from the provisions of the 'Direct Payment Agreement' thereby making them completely autonomous. Such a step may not be feasible in the immediate future as it will certainly be stoutly opposed by the teaching community.

Even if convinced of the economic rationale of the above remedies, the government may, for political reasons, hesitate to implement such a policy. The criticism that the suggested remedies (1) and (2) would jeopardise the legitimate aspirations of the members belonging to the scheduled castes and scheduled tribes and other vulnerable sections of the community for higher education could be met by a liberal policy of scholarships for such sections. Besides, now that government colleges (in all 35) have been established in all but two districts of the state (Pathanamthitta and Alleppey districts do not have government colleges), the interests of the students belonging to the less privileged communities in the matter of education could be taken care of by increasing adequately the existing quota for S.C. and S.T. candidates in these colleges. There is no point in making higher education very cheap for those who can afford to pay their way. Moreover, universal college education unlike universal primary education is not a national goal enshrined in the country's constitution.

Delinking of the private colleges from the

provisions of the 'Direct Payment Agreement' could be effected in different stages and degrees. The government may still opt to provide the colleges a regular grant, albeit a much smaller grant than at present. The colleges would be free to choose the level of tuition fees subject to a suitable ceiling to be fixed by the government from time to time. Similarly the managements would be free to determine the salaries of the teachers they hire subject, of course, to a reasonable minimum. Even now there are several private tutorial colleges — many of the existing aided private colleges are not substantially different from tutorial (parallel) colleges — which prepare and present students for various university examinations. The government has not yet thought of introducing uniform scales of pay for teachers of such institutions on a par with government colleges. The parallel between government hospitals and private hospitals is noteworthy in this context. While doctors employed in some private hospitals are paid much higher salaries (going up to Rs. 10,000-Rs. 12,000 per mensem) than government doctors, there might be others who receive much less. Just as for goods of superior quality one is prepared to pay higher prices, for superior higher education also one must be prepared to pay more. A certain measure of subsidy, however, may be desirable. Rigid standardisation does not lead to excellence in any field, least of all in higher education.

6

EXPENDITURES OF COLLEGES IN THE PRIVATE SECTOR : Patterns and Trends

The main thrust of the present study has been the financing of colleges in the private sector. In keeping with this thrust we have identified, in the two preceding chapters, the different sources of receipts of the private colleges, their relative importance, the trends in the amounts collected from each, both in absolute and relative terms, and the problems arising from the practice, followed by some colleges, of supplementing their receipts from institutional sources with collection through extraneous, and in some cases extra legal, sources such as donations. We now turn to a discussion of the expenditure side. In fact it is from the way colleges allocate their resources that we gain valuable insights into their priorities. It may, however, be noted that since the salaries of the teaching and nonteaching staff are met entirely by the state government, we have not included this item in our discussion of expenditures of colleges. An additional reason for the exclusion of this item consists in the fact that while in respect of government grants for library, laboratory, maintenance of buildings, etc. the actual expenditure incurred by the college during any year may exceed, or fall short of, the grant sanctioned, in respect of salaries of staff, the expenditure incurred exactly matches the sanctioned grant. Needless to say, the colleges have absolutely no discretion regarding the latter.

Expenditures of colleges may be divided into capital expenditures and recurring expenditures. Capital expenditures consist of those on the purchase and improvement of land, construction of buildings, installation of laboratory equipment, purchase of books and journals for the library, purchase of furniture, installation of sanitary and electrical fittings, etc. Expenditure on repair and maintenance of buildings and electrical and sanitary fittings, purchase of chemicals and other perishables for the laboratories, printing, postage and stationery, water, electricity and telephone charges, expenses incurred for the conduct of games and sports, taxes, travelling allowances paid to staff for attending to official work, etc. are included under recurring expenditures.[1] We may, however, reiterate that the limitations of data referred to earlier in connection with our discussion of sources of finance of private colleges are applicable to their expenditures also. For a pioneering work such as the present one, certain gaps in the data are but natural and should not diminish the validity of the analysis and the conclusions emerging therefrom.

1. Capital Expenditure

Acquisition of land and the construction of the minimum essential infrastructure such as buildings and equipment are the primary items of expenditure to be incurred before a college can seek and obtain affiliation and start functioning. Naturally the initiative for these preliminary steps are taken by the sponsoring body and it is most likely that the expenditures incurred on them are not shown in the accounts of the colleges concerned. Further it seems that some managements assume direct responsibility, even after the colleges have started functioning on a firm footing, for major expenditures such as those on buildings. On the other hand, expenditure on libraries and laboratories are more fully reflected in the accounts of the colleges.

In Table 6.1 we present the data on capital expenditures. It is seen that the average capital expenditure per sample college registered a significant increase over time, from Rs. 26,189 in 1972-73 to Rs. 1,34,211 in 1985-86. This increase which forms over 400 per cent is partly explained by the fact that for recent years our data are more complete than for earlier years. Year to year variations in capital expenditure have been considerable, the lowest and the highest expenditures being Rs. 13,990 in 1973-74 and Rs. 1,87,076 in 1984-85 respectively. Though the average capital expenditure per college for the sample as a whole has been rather low, the record of capital expenditure of certain individual colleges during particular periods is seen to have been quite impressive (Table 6.2).

Construction of buildings accounts for the bulk of the relatively large capital expenditures incurred by the eight colleges listed in the table. The extraordinarily huge capital expenditure of St. Mary's College is explained by the fact that it was established in 1981-82 and that a good deal of capital expenditure, mostly on buildings, was undertaken during the first five years of the college's existence.

Among the items of capital expenditure, construction of buildings constitutes the most important. During the period under review, the average annual capital expenditure per sample college on building construction increased from Rs. 11,316 in 1972-73 to Rs. 47,914 in 1985-86. Wide year to year variations in capital expenditure on buildings are observed; thus, from a low of Rs. 4,730 in 1973-74 it reached a high of Rs. 1,06,383 in 1984-85. In terms of proportion to total capital

TABLE 6.1: Average Capital Expenditure Per Sample College, 1972-73 to 1985-86

(Rs.)

Purpose	1972-73	1973-74	1974-75	1975-76	1976-77	1977-78	1978-79
1	2	3	4	5	6	7	8
1. Purchase and improvement of land	2728 (10.4)	57 (0.4)	320 (0.8)	9724 (16.8)	3061 (12.5)	466 (0.7)	1875 (2.3)
2. Construction of new buildings	11316 (43.2)	4730 (33.8)	27382 (66.5)	29762 (51.3)	5204 (21.4)	9502 (28.0)	34242 (43.0)
3. Laboratory equipment	4335 (16.5)	3941 (28.2)	5320 (12.9)	11104 (19.2)	6217 (25.5)	14794 (43.0)	18315 (23.0)
4. Library	5258 (20.1)	3111 (22.2)	3460 (8.4)	4427 (7.6)	5515 (22.6)	8177 (24.0)	17108 (21.5)
5. Furniture and equipment	1430 (5.5)	841 (6.0)	1063 (2.6)	1814 (3.1)	2064 (8.5)	993 (3.0)	7330 (9.2)
6. Sanitary and electrical fittings	523 (2.0)	487 (3.5)	380 (0.9)	561 (1.0)	431 (1.8)	379 (1.1)	335 (0.4)
7. Others	599 (2.3)	823 (5.9)	3275 (7.9)	580 (1.0)	1871 (7.7)	76 (0.2)	456 (0.6)
Total	26189 (100)	13990 (100)	41200(100)	57972(100)	24363(100)	34387(100)	79661(100)

TABLE 6.1 — *Contd.*

(Rs.)

	Purpose	1979-80	1980-81	1981-82	1982-83	1983-84	1984-85	1985-86
	1	9	10	11	12	13	14	15
1.	Purchase and improvement of land	1460 (1.8)	1597 (3.0)	52732 (55.8)	240(0.3)	566(0.5)	1149(0.6)	1248(0.9)
2.	Construction of new buildings	27752 (35.0)	7239 (13.6)	6570 (6.9)	3819347.3)	62965(60.0)	106383(56.9)	47914(35.7)
3.	Laboratory equipment	22583 (28.5)	20658 (38.8)	19108 (20.2)	24856(30.7)	23176(22.1)	37069(19.8)	38670(28.8)
4.	Library	21136 (26.7)	13378 (25.1)	8578 (9.1)	8830(10.9)	10567(10.1)	29374(15.7)	30378(22.6)
5.	Furniture and equipment	3457 (4.4)	2948 (5.5)	5197 (5.5)	5901(7.3)	4204(4.0)	6333(3.4)	12414(9.3)
6.	Sanitary and electrical fittings	790 (1.1)	3082 (5.8)	682 (0.7)	1184(1.5)	796(0.8)	648(0.3)	1456(1.1)
7.	Others	2032 (2.6)	4376 (8.2)	1717 (1.8)	1607(2.0)	2648(2.5)	6120(3.3)	2131(1.6)
	Total	79210(100)	53278(100)	94584(100)	80811(100)	104922(100)	187076(100)	134211(100)

Note : Figures within parentheses refer to percentages.

TABLE 6.2: Average Yearly Capital Expenditure of Selected Colleges, 1972-73 to 1985-86

Name of College	Period	Average annual capital expenditure (Rs. lakh)
1. Mar Ivanios College, Trivandrum	1978-79 to 1979-80 (2 years)	3.86
2. Mar Thoma College, Tiruvalla	1978-79 to 1985-86 (2 years)	2.08
3. Catholicate College, Pathanamthitta	1978-79 to 1982-83 (5 years)	2.25
4. St. Mary's College, Manarcaud	1981-82 to 1985-86 (5 years)	11.14
5. M.S.M. College, Kayamkulam	1979-80 to 1980-81 (2 years)	2.10
6. S.N. College, Quilon	1978-79 to 1985-86 (2 years)	2.27
7. Bishop Moore College, Mavelikara	1984-85 to 1985-86 (2 years)	2.98
8. Payyannur College, Payyannur	1984-85 to 1985-86 (2 years)	3.45

expenditure the relative share of expenditure on buildings was in the range of 7 per cent in 1981-82 to 66.5 per cent in 1974-75. The next important item of capital expenditure is laboratory equipment. Setting up laboratories in science subjects for the various courses is expensive and this fact has prompted many colleges to restrict the number of batches for admission to science groups to the minimum. The average expenditure per sample college on laboratory equipment increased from Rs. 4,335 in 1972-73 to Rs. 38,670 in 1985-86; in terms of relative share, the expenditure per college increased from 16.5 per cent to 28.8 per cent during the same period. During some years the proportion was as high as 43 per cent (1977-78) and in other years, it remained as low as 12.9 per cent (1974-75). While the overall average expenditure on laboratory equipment has been relatively low, certain colleges are seen to have spent exceptionally large amounts. Details of such expenditures are furnished (Table 6.3).

Well-equipped laboratories are an essential input of high-quality education and as such the relatively high expenditure incurred by the above institutions may be indicative of the high standard of education they impart. The data on capital expenditure on laboratories, however, suffer from two limitations : first, for colleges established during the 1940s and 1950s there is a distinct possibility that substantial sums were spent on laboratories during the period prior to 1972-73 the year from which our review begins. Second, from the way accounts are maintained by the colleges it has been impossible in several instances to distinguish capital expenditures on laboratories from recurring expenditures. Hence whatever expenditures which could not clearly be identified as recurring expenditures have been treated as capital expenditures. Thus it is very likely that the capital expenditures reported are somewhat exaggerated.

TABLE 6.3: Average Annual Expenditure on Laboratory Equipment: Selected Colleges, 1972-73 to 1985-86

Name of College	Period	Yearly average expenditure on laboratory equipment (Rs.)
1. M.G. College, Trivandrum	1982-83 to 1985-86 (4 years)	50,577
2. Mar Ivanios College, Trivandrum	1983-84 to 1985-96 (3 years)	56,951
3. Christian College, Kattakada	1977-78 to 1982-83 (6 years)	99,376
4. Mar Thoma College, Tiruvalla	1980-81 to 1985-86 (6 Years)	92,485
5. Catholicate College, Pathanamthitta	1977-78 to 1985-86 (9 years)	61,677
6. S.N. College, Quilon	1982-83 to 1985-86 (4 years)	57,573
7. Payyannur College, Payyannur	1982-83 to 1985-86 (4 years)	53,607
8. Bishop Moore College, Mavelikara	1982-83 to 1985-86 (4 years)	75,801

Besides laboratories, libraries also contribute directly to the quality of education. Under expenditure on libraries we include only expenditure incurred for the purchase of books and periodicals and not expenditure on construction of buildings to house the library. The latter is included in expenditure on buildings. During the period under review, the average expenditure per sample college on libraries increased from Rs. 5,258 in 1972-73 to Rs. 30,019 in 1985-86. In relative terms, expenditure on libraries which formed 20.1 per cent of the capital expenditure in 1972-73, rose to 22.6 per cent in 1985-86. The variations in the relative share of the expenditure on libraries, however, have been rather wide, from 7.6 per cent in 1975-76 to 26.7 per cent in 1979-80. Though, as with expenditure on laboratories, the expenditure per sample college on libraries appears extremely meagre, we should not lose sight of the fact that a few colleges have made it a point to set apart much larger funds for the purpose as shown in Table 6.4

TABLE 6.4: Average Annual Capital Expenditure on Libraries: Selected Colleges, 1972-73 to 1985-86

Name of College	Period	Average annual expenditure (Rs.)
1. Mar Ivanios College, Trivandrum	1978-79 to 1985-86 (8 years)	66,796
2. Mar Thoma College, Tiruvalla	1978-79 to 1985-86 (8 years)	87,687
3. Catholicate College, Pathanamthitta	1978-79 to 1981-82 (4 years)	86,249
4. S.N. College, Quilon	1980-81 to 1985-86 (6 years)	70,186

Considering the ever-growing enrolment, the number of courses and the subjects offered as well as the cost of standard publications, the amounts shown under this item of expenditure cannot be said to be adequate.

Of the remaining items of capital expenditure, there is only one, namely furniture and equipment, which is significant. The average expenditure per college on this item increased from Rs. 1,430 in 1972-73 to Rs. 12,414 in 1985-86. In relative terms the share of this item of expenditure rose from 5.5 per cent to 9.3 per cent during the same period.

Purchase and improvement of land is not usually a significant item of expenditure as it is in most cases only a once-and-for-all expenditure. Subsequently it may become an important item if and when a college goes in for the purchase of size-able area of land for construction of additional buildings, provision of playgrounds or approach roads.

The preceding discussion is based on fragmentary evidence since for many colleges the management assumes responsibility for meeting many of the capital expenditures. Such expenditures are not reflected in the accounts of the colleges concerned. The total amounts incurred by colleges under capital expenditure are, therefore, likely to be higher than those shown in the tables presented in this section.

2. Recurring Expenditure

Besides capital expenditure, colleges in their normal functioning have also to incur several types of recurring expenditures such as those on maintenance and repair of buildings, electrical and sanitary installations, vehicles, campus roads, garden, etc., purchase of chemicals and other materials for laboratories; stationery, printing and postage, water, electricity and telephone charges; conduct of sports and games; payment of taxes, travel expenses of staff, etc. (Table 6.5).

The average recurring expenditure per sample college increased from Rs. 24,334 in 1972-73 to Rs. 66,473 in 1985-86. The highest average recurring expenditure of Rs. 74,807 was registered in 1984-85. Among the different items of recurring expenditures, repairs and maintenance is the most prominent. During the 14-year period under review, the average annual expenditure per sample college on this item amounted to Rs. 11,352. It increased from Rs. 5,319 (21.9%) in 1972-73 to Rs. 19,198 (28.9%) in 1985-86. The range of variation in the

TABLE 6.5: Average Recurring Expenditure Per Sample College, 1972-73 to 1985-86

(Rs.)

Purpose	1972-73	1973-74	1974-75	1975-76	1976-77	1977-78	1978-79
1	2	3	4	5	6	7	8
1. Repair and maintenance	5319 (21.9)	5892 (24.0)	9713 (29.4)	6954 (19.1)	5875 (15.6)	8845 (22.5)	11052 (27.7)
2. Chemicals and materials for laboratories	5551 (22.8)	6664 (27.2)	7606 (23.0)	10019 (27.6)	11267 (29.8)	7963 (20.3)	5500 (13.8)
3. Stationery Printing and Postage	2818 (11.6)	2681 (10.9)	3817 (11.5)	4368 (12.0)	5086 (13.5)	4980 (12.7)	5727 (14.3)
4. Water, electricity & telephone charges	1717 (7.1)	1877 (7.7)	2633 (8.0)	2967 (8.2)	2328 (6.2)	2519 (6.4)	2518 (6.3)
5. Sports and games	3534 (14.5)	5306 (21.6)	6823 (20.6)	9462 (26.0)	9397 (24.9)	11501 (29.3)	11723 (29.4)
6. Travelling allowances	4068 (16.7)	811 (3.3)	1054 (3.2)	990 (2.7)	710 (1.9)	772 (2.0)	1260 (3.2)
7. Others	1327 (5.4)	1302 (5.3)	1404 (4.3)	1590 (4.4)	3067 (8.1)	2676 (6.8)	2136 (5.3)
Total	24334(100)	24533(100)	33050(100)	36350(100)	37730(100)	39256(100)	39916(100)

TABLE 6.5 — *Contd.*

Purpose	1979-80	1980-81	1981-82	1982-83	1983-84	1984-85	1985-86
1	9	10	11	12	13	14	15
1. Repair and maintenance	19591 (34.4)	13718 (29.2)	9925 (21.2)	11274 (21.2)	17489 (26.4)	14092 (18.8)	19198 (28.9)
2. Chemicals and materials for laboratories	8349 (14.7)	8793 (18.7)	6824 (14.5)	14126 (26.6)	16271 (24.6)	18595 (24.9)	15495 (23.3)
3. Stationery Printing and Postage	7577 (13.3)	5447 (11.6)	7221 (15.4)	6825 (12.8)	9876 (14.9)	12955 (17.3)	7249 (10.9)
4. Water, electricity & telephone charges	3369 (5.9)	3018 (6.4)	3829 (8.2)	4154 (7.8)	4862 (7.3)	7564 (10.1)	7431 (11.2)
5. Sports and games	14681 (25.7)	12761 (27.2)	15120 (32.3)	13206 (24.9)	13612 (20.5)	16349 (21.8)	13987 (21.0)
6. Travelling allowances	1220 (2.1)	1287 (2.7)	1577 (3.4)	1203 (2.3)	1343 (2.0)	1609 (2.2)	1329 (2.7)
7. Others	2205 (3.9)	1975 (4.2)	2365 (5.0)	2314 (4.4)	2838 (4.3)	3643 (4.9)	1784 (2.7)
Total	56992(100)	46999(100)	46861(100)	53102(100)	66291(100)	74807(100)	66473(100)

Note : Figures within parentheses refer to percentages.

relative share of this item was from 15.6 per cent in 1976-77 to 34.4 per cent in 1979-80. As noted earlier since maintenance grants are not received from the government promptly, several colleges do not undertake maintenance of buildings on a regular basis. In a few cases it is possible that the managements assume direct responsibility for meeting this important need. In any case, from the way college buildings look it is evident that maintenance is neglected in most cases. The only exceptions are a few well-established colleges like Guruvayurappan College, Calicut; Mar Ivanios College, Trivandrum, Fatima Mata National College and Sree Narayana College, Quilon. During the three-year period from 1983-84 to 1985-86, these colleges spent on the average Rs. 46,440, Rs. 22,012, Rs. 42,563 and Rs. 1,05,098 per year respectively on maintenance and repairs. The next most important item of recurring expenditure is purchase of chemicals and materials for the laboratories. The average amount spent on this item during the period under review was Rs. 10,216 per sample college. Expenditure on this item increased from Rs. 5,551 (22.8%) in 1972-73 to Rs. 15,495 (23.3%) in 1985-86. Year-to-year variations in these expenditures have been considerable; in absolute terms it varied from Rs. 5,500 in 1978-79 to Rs. 18,595 in 1984-85 and in relative terms from 13.8 per cent in 1978-79 to 27.6 per cent in 1975-76. We may recall here a certain limitation of our data pertaining to expenditure on laboratories pointed out earlier, namely the failure of the sample colleges to keep capital expenditures separate from recurring expenditures. It is pointed out that the laboratory fees collected from the students are insufficient to defray the full cost of chemicals and materials. Some colleges depend, therefore, on their Parent-Teacher Associations for additional funds.

An item of recurring expenditure which is of considerable importance is sports and games. In fact over the years a steady increase in the expenditure on this item is noted in abosolute as well as relative terms. Thus the average annual recurring expenditure per sample college on sports and games increased from Rs. 3,534 (14.50%) in 1972-73 to Rs. 13,987 (21%) in 1985-86. In several years the proportion had risen well above 25 per cent. It is interesting to note that a few colleges have been spending consistently large amounts on sports and games. Thus during the 5-year period from 1981-82 to 1985-86, M.G. College spent on an average Rs. 40,632, N.S.S. College, Nilamel, Rs. 22,651; Catholicate College, Pathanamthitta, Rs. 24,793; St. Paul's College, Kalamasserry, Rs. 21,937; St. Thomas College, Trichur, Rs. 31,690 (average for four years only) and Payyannur College Rs. 30,303. Such increased spending may be the outcome of a new awareness of the importance of sports and games. It may, however, be added that what is shown as recurring expenditure on sports and games may be actually capital expenditure - a problem we have already confronted in connection with expenditures on laboratories.

The above three items of expenditures account for almost three-fourths of the total recurring expenditures of the sample colleges. The remaining four items including 'miscellaneous expenditures' form only one-fourth of the total. They are routine items and do not directly contribute to the academic and athletic performance of the colleges.

The foregoing discussion on the expenditures of the sample colleges was made in terms of capital expenditures and recurring expenditures. However, as we have already cautioned, meticulous care might not have been exercised by the colleges concerned in applying this distinction in the actual accounting of the various expenditures. Consequently there is much likelihood of some recurring expenditures being recorded as capital expenditures and *vice versa*. To overcome such distortions, we may

TABLE 6.6: Average Total Expenditure Per Sample College 1972-73 to 1985-86

(Rs. lakhs)

1972-73	1973-74	1974-75	1975-76	1976-77	1977-78	1978-79	1979-80	1980-81	1981-82	1982-83	1983-84	1984-85	1985-86
1	2	3	4	5	6	7	8	9	10	11	12	13	14
0.51	0.39	0.74	0.94	0.62	0.74	1.20	1.36	1.00	1.41	1.34	1.71	2.62	2.01

combine the two expenditures and treat them as the total expenditures of the colleges. Even then the figures may not give a correct account of the expenditures of the colleges for the reasons already mentioned, namely (1) gaps in the data and (2) direct provision of several expenditures by the management. The combined expenditures of the sample colleges for the period under review are presented in Table 6.6.

As already pointed out, we have excluded the payment of salaries to the teaching and nonteaching staff from our computation of the average expenditure per sample college as salaries are now paid directly by the government through its treasury. Our analysis of the expenditures of the sample colleges has clearly shown that, net of payment of salaries of the staff, most colleges spend only paltry sums on the upkeep of the institutions; the accent is on survival and not on development or excellence. With such meagre allotments, the outcome is easily predictable. In the next chapter we turn our attention to examining the differential academic performance of the sample colleges.

NOTE

1. Expenditures have been classified into 'capital' and 'recurring' broadly on the basis of their end products. Capital expenditures are those which lead to the creation of assets such as land, building, equipment, etc. On the other hand, recurring expenditures do not result in the production of any assets. Besides, such expenditures are of a recurring nature. Purchase of chemicals and other perishables for the laboratories, printing, postage and stationery, water, electricity and telephone bills, etc. are good examples of recurring expenditures. In respect of certain expenditures, as, for example, those on furniture and library, however, one might doubt whether they are capital or recurring. Furniture as an item of household expenditure is treated as consumer durables along with domestic appliances. However, in any production unit (engaged in the production of a good or service) expenditure

on furniture forms a capital item. The same is true of expenditure on library. Both furniture and library form parts of the essential physical infrastructure required for the imparting of instruction. Of course, not all book and journals added to the library are of equal value as instruments of education; while some titles may be widely used, others may remain little used. But this is a different matter.

7

PERFORMANCE AND PROSPECT: Interrelationship Between Financial and Non-financial Factors

Our discussion in the preceding chapters has brought out several deficiencies in the field of college education in the private sector in Kerala. The major concern of the government seems to have been merely to keep the colleges going by making payments regularly of the salaries of the academic and administrative staff; no serious effort is seen to have gone into from any quarter to update and upgrade the standard of instruction so as to improve the quality of the various inputs which contribute to excellence in education. During the pre-Independence period there existed only a very limited number of Arts and Science colleges in Kerala. Whether in the public sector or in the private sector, those colleges had maintained a reputation for good performance. They were staffed by eminent teachers and among the graduates who came out of the portals of such colleges were scores of well known personalities who made their mark in the vocations of their choice. The scene has changed vastly since then. The period since Independence has witnessed political turbulence and growing rivalry among different socio-economic pressure groups. It was, however, a period which witnessed proliferation of Arts and Science colleges in the private sector. The successive governments which came to power in Kerala were keen to maintain the balance among the different communities – an obsession which has reflected itself even in the sanctioning of new colleges. In the process, the criterion of genuine educational requirements took the back seat. Such proliferation has naturally led to a lowering of the standards of basic facilities since resources of the state had to be very thinly spread over an ever increasing number of colleges. This fact is reflected in the low expenditures incurred on libraries and laboratories. Apart from the inadequacy of the educational infrastructure, non-academic factors also have led to the lowering of standards. In this chapter we shall attempt an evaluation of the sample colleges on the basis of a few selected academic norms and try to find out the way their interrelationships have in combination contributed to the observed deterioration. A few general comments about some of the more conspicuous non-academic factors that have adversely affected the quality of college education may be in order before we venture into this analysis.

Unionisation of Teachers

We have earlier noted that systematic unionisation of college teachers and the series of agitations launched under the auspices of such unions enabled the teaching community to wrest from the managements and the government many a right, the Direct Payment Agreement being their culmination. During the days when teachers were appointed by the college managements and their salaries directly disbursed by the principal, the teachers had a more direct and personal relationship with the management; not only were teachers in those days more loyal to the college, they had also a greater sense of commitment to the cause of higher education. In other words there existed a sort of partnership between the management and the teachers. The introduction of direct payment of salaries through the government treasury and the appointment of teachers, in several cases, on payment of donations have led to a certain degree of alienation of the teaching community from the management; the direct personal ties between the teachers and the management have snapped. In this transition the management has to a large extent also lost control over the teachers. Further the organisation of college teachers along trade union lines with pronounced political affiliations has led to a further cleavage between the two parties. The teachers' organisations, because of their political clout, are confident that they could face up to any challenge thrown up by the management. All these developments have meant that the close identity of interests that once existed between the management and the teachers have, with rare exceptions, totally disappeared.

Existence of Multiple Unions of Teachers

The academic atmosphere of the colleges has become vitiated further by the fact that instead of the entire body of teachers of a given college being members of one and the same organisation, their membership lies dispersed in several unions. For instance, once a monolithic and strong organisation, the AKPCTA (All Kerala Private College Teachers' Association) has split into two rival factions; so is PCTA (Private College Teachers' Association), another organisation owing allegiance to non-Marxist political parties. The splits have meant that whenever an agitation is launched by either the teachers or the students there is likely to ensue some 'joint action' by students' and teachers' organisations which have political sympathies with the agitators. In the event, it is the cause of higher education which suffers as a result of such internecine conflicts within the academic community.

Time-bound Promotions

Another factor that has had an adverse impact on the scholastic attitudes and academic competence of the teaching community is the system of non-cadre promotions – promotions of lecturers to second grade and first grade professors, based merely on length of service. Since such promotions are not at all based on professional attainments, teachers in private colleges – and this is equally true of government colleges – have in general lost the urge to improve their qualifications or update their teaching equipment. Lately, as a result of the Faculty Improvement Programme (FIP) implemented by the University Grants Commission, teachers have, however, begun to evince some interest in improving their qualifications. Unfortunately this otherwise welcome change is confined to a few colleges, partly because not all managements are seen to have been keen and having the initiative to take advantage of the UGC assistance.[1]

Engagement of Teachers in Other Avocations

The college atmosphere has become still further vitiated by the fact that some teachers have taken to other avocations such as private tuition, trade, transport, printing and publishing, etc., in order to supplement their income. Though such teachers are supposed to be whole-time members of the teaching staff drawing full salary, in effect they are only part-time teachers. One might take consolation in the fact that such teachers still form only a minority but their tribe is on the increase in spite of the existence of definite clauses in the service rules which prohibit such involvement. Undoubtedly such persons are largely responsible for lowering the prestige of the teaching profession in the eyes of the public. Incidentally, this malady is not confined to teachers in private colleges; it is prevalent among teachers in government colleges as well. Apart from carrying on such lucrative avocations, many teachers (in private colleges) also hold office in political parties or their feeder organisations. Thus we have today private college teachers who are state ministers, trade union leaders or office bearers of political parties at the local, taluk, district and state levels. A third category of teacher-politicians consists of those actively involved in the running of local government organs – panchayats, municipalities and corporations – in different capacities as members, councillors or presiding officers. In short, today there are college teachers of different hues; it is becoming increasingly difficult to identify a 'pure' college teacher.

Performance of Colleges : Examination Results

Having outlined some of the more conspicuous non-academic factors that have led to the lowering of standards of college education in the private sector, we now attempt an assessment of the performance of the sample colleges. Since colleges are engaged mainly in imparting instruction at the predegree,[2] degree and postgraduate levels, the performance of a college may be judged in terms of its examination results. Besides examination results, one should take into account, strictly speaking, its research output also. However, since the vast majority of the colleges in Kerala concentrates on teaching and that too at the predegree and degree levels, we may attempt an evaluation of the performance of the colleges in terms of examination results only.[3] The predegree results of the sample colleges for 1984-85 and 1985-86 and the averages for the two years are given in Table 7.1.

TABLE 7.1: Performance of Sample Colleges: Results of Predegree Examinations (March-April), 1985 and 1986

Sl. No. Name of College	1985			1986			Average for	
	No. presented	No. passed	No. passed in I class	No. presented	No. passed	No. passed in I class	1985 Pass (percentage)	1986 I class (percentage)
1	2	3	4	5	6	7	8	9
1. Mahatma Gandhi	648	161	17	720	175	16	24.6	2.4
2. Mar Ivanios	628	489	227	733	557	274	76.9	36.8
3. Christian, Kattakada	1030	240	40	1032	270	74	24.7	5.5
4. N.S.S., Nilamel	805	233	29	680	238	33	33.6	4.2
5. T.K.M.M. College	734	201	38	754	214	97	27.9	9.1
6. St. Aloysius	596	225	8	660	229	26	36.1	2.7
7. Mar Thoma	861	388	102	868	381	81	44.5	10.6
8. F.M.N. College	860	449	136	857	366	124	47.5	15.1
9. Catholicate	780	289	62	797	349	73	40.4	8.6
10. St. Mary's	235	29	—	293	57	—	16.3	—
11. St. Paul's	697	259	89	762	405	117	45.5	14.1

(Contd.)

TABLE 7.1 — *(Contd.)*

1	2	3	4	5	6	7	8	9
12. S.D. College	764	274	66	742	309	69	38.7	9.0
13. St. Thomas	837	538	296	852	581	242	66.3	31.9
14. MES Ponnani	501	263	32	509	280	39	53.8	7.0
15. MSM College	870	201	29	843	236	43	25.5	4.2
16. Guruvayurappan	452	145	30	418	142	24	33.0	6.2
17. Nirmalagiri	592	407	160	618	428	173	69.0	27.5
18. NSS, Manjeri	518	127	33	418	140	16	28.5	5.2
19. S.N., Quilon	606	218	65	756	307	98	38.5	12.1
20. S.N., Chelannur	N A	N A	N A	N A	N A	N A	N A	N A
21. Payyannur college	758	349	133	699	326	112	46.3	16.8
22. Bishop Moore	612	376	99	568	248	107	52.9	17.5
23. D.B. College	1113	406	83	1349	414	87	33.3	6.9
24. Sir Syed	726	245	52	671	228	47	33.9	7.0
25. St. Michael's	706	235	74	719	287	95	36.6	11.9
All colleges	16929	6747	1900	17318	7167	2067	40.6	11.6

Source: Data furnished by the sample colleges.
N A = Not Available

The percentage of pass is taken as a measure of the relative performance of the colleges. On the basis of the average results of the predegree examinations of 1985 and 1986 (March-April), the names of the colleges with a pass-percentage above the sample average are given in Table 7.2 (in the descending order). Along with the ranking on the basis of the percentage of pass, we also give their ranks on the basis of percentage of first class. It is observed that generally there is a direct relationship between percentage of pass and percentage of first class.

TABLE 7.2: Ranking of Sample Colleges with Above-average Performance: Predegree Examination Results (Average for 1985 and 1986)

Name of college	Rank	Percentage of pass	Percentage of I Class
Mar Ivanios	1	76.9	36.8
Nirmalagiri	2	69.0	27.5
St. Thomas	3	66.3	31.9
M.E.S., Ponnani	4	53.8	7.0
Bishop Moore	5	52.9	17.5
F.M.N., Quilon	6	47.5	15.1
Payyannur College	7	46.3	16.8
St. Paul's	8	45.5	14.1
Mar Thoma	9	44.5	10.6
Sample Average		40.6	11.6

Of the nine colleges, six are in the Travancore-Cochin region and three in the Malabar region; three colleges are under the Kerala University, two under the Mahatma Gandhi University and four under the Calicut University. Obviously the nine colleges with above-average performance in the predegree examination are unevenly distributed among the three universities as well as the two regions.

TABLE 7.3: Performance of Sample Colleges: Results of Degree Examinations (March-April), 1985 and 1986

Sl. No.	Name of College	1985			1986			Average for	
		No. pre-sented	No. pass-ed	No. pass-ed in I class	No. pre-sented	No. pass-ed	No. pass-ed in I class	1985 Pass (per-cent-age)	1986 I class (per-cent-age)
	1	2	3	4	5	6	7	8	9
1.	Mahatma Gandhi	276	158	42	284	116	40	48.9	14.6
2.	Mar Ivanios	300	229	102	288	205	81	73.8	31.1
3.	Christian, Kattakada	242	117	29	191	121	68	55.0	22.4
4.	N.S.S. Nilamel	243	152	17	284	159	21	59.0	7.2
5.	T.K.M.M. College	226	107	29	200	143	23	58.6	12.2
6.	St. Aloysius	96	69	21	69	42	13	67.3	20.6
7.	Mar Thoma	245	187	85	286	214	80	87.4	36.0
8.	F.M.N. College	411	250	91	439	268	99	60.9	22.4
9.	Catholicate	287	182	69	306	219	57	67.6	21.2
10.	St. Mary's	—	—	—	—	—	—	—	—
11.	St. Paul's	112	63	24	103	77	17	65.1	19.1

(Contd.)

TABLE 7.3 — *(Contd.)*

1	2	3	4	5	6	7	8	9
12. S.D. College	434	169	34	419	184	41	41.4	8.8
13. St. Thomas	389	225	75	376	257	93	63.0	22.0
14. M.E.S. Ponnani	129	74	12	126	70	8	56.5	7.8
15. M.S.M. College	277	168	47	395	231	62	59.4	16.2
16. Guruvayurappan	276	148	38	266	169	42	58.5	14.8
17. Nirmalagiri	176	168	86	147	140	89	95.4	54.2
18. N.S.S. Manjeri	121	48	13	131	78	24	50.0	14.7
19. S.N. College, Quilon	238	152	41	324	229	42	67.8	14.8
20. S.N. College, Chelannur	134	75	20	127	67	15	54.4	13.4
21. Payyannur College	290	230	80	341	286	94	81.8	27.6
22. Bishop Moore	257	161	84	249	201	66	71.5	29.6
23. Devaswom Board College	443	101	36	436	98	38	22.6	8.4
24. Sir Syed	211	139	53	187	125	47	66.3	25.1
25. St. Michael's	88	57	21	76	59	16	70.0	22.6
All	5901	3429	1149	6050	3758	1176	60.1	19.4

Source: Data furnished by the colleges.
Note: St. Mary's College does not have degree courses.

It will be interesting to examine if the order of ranking observed at the predegree examination is retained at the degree examinations also. Table 7.3 shows the results of the B.A./B.Sc./B.Com. examinations for 1985 and 1986. Again, on the basis of the average results of the degree examinations of 1985 and 1986 (March-April) the ranking of the colleges with above-average performance is given in Table 7.4 (in the descending order). Of the thirteen colleges thus ranked, ten are in the Travancore-Cochin region and three in the Malabar region; five colleges are under the Kerala University, four under the Mahatma Gandhi University and four under the Calicut University.

TABLE 7.4: Ranking of Sample Colleges with Above-average Performance: Degree Examinations (Average for 1985 and 1986)

Name of college	Rank	Percentage of pass	Percentage of I Class
Nirmalagiri	1	95.4	54.2
Mar Thoma	2	87.4	36.0
Payyannur College	3	81.8	27.6
Mar Ivanios	4	73.8	31.1
Bishop Moore	5	71.5	29.6
St. Michael's	6	70.7	22.6
S.N., Quilon	7	67.8	14.8
Catholicate	8	67.6	21.2
St. Aloysius	9	67.3	20.6
Sir Syed	10	66.3	25.1
St. Paul's	11	65.1	19.1
St. Thomas	12	63.0	22.0
F.M.N., Quilon	13	60.9	22.4
Sample Average		60.1	19.4

It is interesting to note that all the colleges except one, namely M.E.S. College, Ponnani, whose performance was above average at the predegree examination figure also among the colleges which had above-average performance to their credit at the degree examinations. It may also however be instructive to examine how the sample colleges in general compare with respect to their performance at different university examinations. Since all the colleges in our sample do not offer postgraduate courses, we may restrict such a comparison to predegree and degree examinations. The relative ranks of the sample colleges at the two examinations are given in Table 7.5.

TABLE 7.5: Relative Performance of Sample Colleges: Predegree and Degree Examinations, 1985 and 1986

Name of College	Rank according to percentage of Pass		Difference
	Predegree	Degree	
Mar Ivanios	1	4	-3
Nirmalagiri	2	1	1
St. Thomas	3	12	-9
M.E.S. Ponnani	4	18	-14
Bishop Moore	5	5	0
F.M.N. Quilon	6	13	-7
Payyannur College	7	3	4
St. Paul's	8	11	-3
Mar Thoma	9	2	7
Catholicate	10	8	2
S.D. College	11	22	-11
S.N., Quilon	12	7	5
St. Michael's	13	6	7
St. Aloysius	14	9	5
Sir Syed	15	10	5
N.S.S., Nilamel	16	15	1
D.B. College	17	23	-6
Guruvayurappan	18	17	1
N.S.S., Manjeri	19	20	-1
T.K.M.M. College	20	16	4
M.S.M. College	21	14	7
Christian College	22	19	3
Mahatma Gandhi	23	21	2
		Rank correlation = 0.62	

Note: Two of the sample colleges are excluded from the table because St. Mary's College does not have degree courses and Predegree results of S.N. College, Chelannur, are not available.

It will be noted that the maximum difference possible between the two rankings in a sample of 23 is 22 (plus or minus). It is seen that except in the case of two colleges, namely M.E.S., Ponnani and S.D. College, the difference between the predegree and degree ranks is 9 or less. We may, therefore, conclude that generally speaking colleges which do well in one University examination repeat approximately the same performance in other examinations too. (The estimated rank correlation of 0.62 is found to be significant.)

Our sample contains only fifteen colleges having postgraduate courses; we have, however, data on results of postgraduate examinations only for 14 of them. The data are presented in Table 7.6. On the basis of the average results of the postgraduate examinations of 1985 and 1986, the ranking of the sample colleges with above-average performance is given in Table 7.7 (in the descending order). In this context it is pertinent to note that students undergoing postgraduate courses generally do not aim at a mere pass in the examination; they aim at securing a class, preferably a first class. The performance of a college in postgraduate examinations may, therefore, be judged in terms of the percentage of first class.

It is seen that of the 14 colleges offering postgraduate courses, only five colleges had a percentage of first class above the sample average of 32.3. Among them, Bishop Moore, Mar Ivanios and Mar Thoma had done well in terms of percentage of pass in the predegree and degree examinations also. Both Catholicate College and S.N. College, Quilon, did well in the degree examinations but not so in the predegree examination. It is thus evident that there are marked differences in the performance of the sample colleges. These differences could be due to various factors such as the quality of the teachers, calibre of the students admitted, library and laboratory facilities, discipline prevailing on the

TABLE 7.6: Performance of Sample Colleges: Results of Postgraduate Examinations (March-April), 1985 and 1986

Sl. No.	Name of College	1985			1986			Average for	
		No. presented	No. passed	No. passed in I class	No. presented	No. passed	No. passed in I class	1985 Pass (percentage)	1986 I class (percentage)
1.	Mahatma Gandhi	66	61	23	62	54	18	89.8	32.0
2.	Mar Ivanios	64	50	27	71	57	30	79.3	42.2
3.	Mar Thoma	64	52	25	78	61	23	79.6	33.8
4.	F.M.N., Quilon	95	59	25	91	77	27	73.1	28.0
5.	Catholicate	77	77	27	92	47	56	73.4	49.1
6.	St. Paul's	13	9	—	23	23	6	88.9	16.7
7.	St. Thomas	89	69	28	110	59	28	64.3	28.4
8.	M.E.S., Ponnani	13	13	3	20	13	1	78.8	12.1
9.	Guruvayurappan	44	37	9	44	39	8	86.4	19.3
10.	S.N., Quilon	162	156	64	171	150	56	91.9	36.0
11.	Bishop Moore	11	7	4	10	9	5	76.2	42.8
12.	D.B. College	21	16	2	27	11	1	56.3	6.3
13.	Sir Syed	11	11	1	18	15	4	89.7	17.2
14.	M.S.M. College	25	20	8	36	25	11	73.8	31.1
	All colleges	755	637	246	853	640	274	79.4	32.3

college campus, extent of loss of working days due to strikes and agitations, etc. It has not been possible in the present study to probe into all such factors, partly because in respect of variables such as discipline, calibre of students, etc., there is a problem of measurement and partly because in respect of quantifiable variables such as expenditure on laboratories, detailed (stage-wise) data are hard to come by. Since the number of science courses/subjects offered varies from college to college and also as there are significant differences between the laboratory requirements of different science courses/subjects (e.g. Botany and Chemistry), a mere comparison of the total expenditure on laboratories per college does not help us draw valid inference regarding the adequacy of the standard of the laboratories. We are, therefore, constrained to focus attention on two of the variables only, namely (1) quality of faculty and (2) library.

TABLE 7.7: Ranking of Sample Colleges with Above-average Performance: Postgraduate Examinations (Average of 1985 and 1986)

Sl. No.	Name of college	Rank	Percentage of I Class
1.	Catholicate College	1	49.1
2.	Bishop Moore	2	42.8
3.	Mar Ivanios	3	42.2
4.	S.N., Quilon	4	36.0
5.	Mar Thoma	5	33.8
Sample average			32.3

Quality of Faculty

For the purpose of our analysis, superior quality of the faculty is measured in terms of higher (research) degrees such as M.Phil. and Ph.D. We assume that teachers with higher degrees prove to be of greater competence in teaching and that the existence of such good teachers, in turn, attract better students to the colleges concerned.

In contrast to the situation in many prestigious colleges in the private sector in the rest of the country, colleges in Kerala do not have many Ph.Ds on their faculty. In recent years, however, a greater awareness on the part of the college teachers of the need for equipping themselves with additional (research) degrees such as Ph.D. and M.Phil. is discernible thanks to the Faculty Improvement Programme of the University Grants Commission. In Table 7.8 we present data on the number of teachers of sample colleges having research degrees. The number mentioned are those which were reported to us during the time of investigation. Some additions and deletions might have taken place since then.

On the average the number of teachers with research degrees (Ph.D. or m.Phil) works out to 6.7 per cent of their total number. Out of the 25 sample colleges 8 had percentages of teachers with research degrees above the sample average of 6.7. Compared to the prestigious private colleges in the rest of the country,[4] the percentage of teachers having research degrees especially, Ph.D. is very low in colleges in the private sector in Kerala. Apart from the percentage of Ph.Ds in any college being very small, there are only a few colleges which have more than one Ph.D. in the same department. Among the colleges which enjoy such a distinction, mention may be made of Mar Thoma College, Mahatma Gandhi College, Mar Ivanios College, S.N. College (Quilon), S.D. College, Catholicate College, St. Paul's College and F.M.N. College. The distribution of teachers with Ph.Ds among different departments of these college is given in Table 7.9.

Among these colleges only the first six are privileged to have more than one department with a minimum of two Ph.Ds on the faculty. We earlier referred to certain prestigious private colleges

TABLE 7.8: Quality of the Teachers: Ranking of Sample Colleges (Descending Order) According to the Percentage of Teachers with Research Degrees, 1986-1988

Rank	Name of college	No. of teachers	No. of Ph.Ds	No. of M. Phils	Total. No. of teachers with research degrees	Percentage of teachers with research degrees
1.	Mar Thoma	147	15	8	23	15.6
2.	Mahatma Gandhi	148	16	6	22	14.9
3.	Mar Ivanios	136	7	12	19	14.0
4.	Catholicate	150	10	7	17	11.3
5.	S.N., Quilon	185	8	12	20	10.8
6.	S.D. College	150	9	6	15	10.0
7.	Bishop Moore	101	2	7	9	8.9
8.	St. Mary's	29	—	2	2	6.9
9.	F.M.N., Quilon	149	6	4	10	6.7
10.	Christian, Kattakada	105	2	5	7	6.7
11.	St. Paul's	82	4	1	5	6.1
12.	S.N., Chelannur	51	—	3	3	6.0
13.	St. Thomas	154	5	3	8	5.2
14.	Payyannur college	118	2	4	6	5.1
15.	Guruvayurappan	116	4	1	5	4.3
16.	Sir Syed, College	107	2	2	4	3.7
17.	M.S.M., College	161	2	4	6	3.7
18.	Nirmalagiri	86	2	—	2	2.3
19.	T.K.M.M. College	92	—	2	2	2.2
20.	N.S.S., Nilamel	94	1	1	2	2.1
21.	D.B. College	145	1	1	2	1.4
22.	St. Aloysius	82	—	1	1	1.2
23.	M.E.S., Ponnani	84	—	—	—	—
24.	N.S.S., Manjeri	80	—	—	—	—
25.	St. Michael's	65	—	—	—	—
	All colleges	2817	98	92	190	6.7

TABLE 7.9: Inter-departmental Distribution of Teachers with Ph.Ds, Selected Sample Colleges, 1986-88

Sl. No.	Name of College	Names of departments with 2 or more Ph.Ds								
		English	Malayalam	Hindi	Physics	Chemistry	Zoology	Botany	Economics	Sociology
1.	Mar Thoma	2	—	2	3	2	—	2	—	—
2.	Mahatma Gandhi	—	2	2	5	—	2	2	—	2
3.	Mar Ivanios	—	—	—	—	3	2	—	—	—
4.	S.N., Quilon	—	—	—	—	2	—	2	—	—
5.	S.D., Alleppey	—	—	3	—	—	—	2	2	—
6.	Catholicate	—	2	2	—	2	—	—	—	—
7.	St. Paul's	—	—	—	2	—	—	—	—	—
8.	F.M.N., Quilon	—	—	—	—	—	2	—	—	—

outside Kerala having more than 50 per cent of the faculty with Ph.Ds. It should, however, be remembered that all those colleges without a single exception are very old institutions – in most cases over hundred years old. All of them invariably had humble beginnings and it took them many decades of dedicated and tireless effort to attain their present stature. Viewed in this perspective, the top colleges in our sample should also be considered to have the potential to grow into premier institutions. The question which remains would be whether the required objective conditions do exist.

Interestingly, most of the colleges with relatively strong faculties have done well in the university examinations, the only exception being the S.N. College, Quilon. This college which occupied the fifth place in terms of the percentage of teachers with research degrees has fallen far behind in terms of the percentage of pass (as well as the percentage of first class) in the university examinations.

Library Facilities

Apart from the quality of the faculty, the academic performance of a college is also influenced by the library facilities. Since library facilities are determined not only by the number of titles available but also by the number of users, we present the title – student ratio as a measure of the library facilities (Table 7.10).

We note that most of the colleges which had a title-student ratio above the sample average of 9.7 in general performed well in the university examinations. Similarly most of the colleges with lower title-student ratios than the sample average have been poor performers. Our analysis has thus shown, with a few exceptions, that there is a positive relationship between library facilities and academic performance. The relationship observed is not, however, very close. In comparing the library facilities offered by the sample colleges we should bear in mind the limitation of the information used, namely the number of titles. By acquiring multiple copies of low-priced books it is always possible to inflate the size of the collection. Such short-cuts are often resorted to by colleges, especially the newly-started ones, in order to fulfil the requirements of affiliation stipulated by the university. However, the more serious-minded managements are likely to keep the academic objectives above narrow financial considerations.

TABLE 7.10: Library Facilities of the Sample Colleges as on 31st March, 1986 (ranked in the descending order)

Name of college	Title-student ratio	Rank
S.N., Quilon	19.1	1
Bishop Moore	18.8	2
Mar Ivanios	14.6	3
Guruvayurappan	14.3	4
Nirmalagiri	14.0	5
Mar Thoma	13.4	6
F.M.N. College	13.0	7
St. Thomas	12.8	8
Catholicate	12.4	9
Sir Syed	8.6	10
Mahatma Gandhi	8.3	11
St. Paul's	8.2	12
S.D. College	7.5	13
M.E.S., Ponnani	7.5	14
Payyannur College	7.3	15
N.S.S., Manjeri	7.0	16
N.S.S., Nilamel	6.8	17
D.B. College	5.3	18
Christian, Kattakada	5.1	19
M.S.M. College	4.9	20
St. Michael's	4.9	21
T.K.M.M. College	4.3	22
St. Mary's	3.6	23
St. Aloysius	1.5	24
S.N., Chelannur	N.A.	
All colleges	9.7	

N.A. = Not Available

It may also be pertinent to note that the colleges with high title-student ratios with a few exceptions like Bishop Moore and Nirmalagiri (both started in 1964) are among the oldest colleges in the State. An examination of Tables 7.8 and 7.10 shows that generally colleges which have a large percentage of teachers with research degrees also maintain good libraries. Six of the sample colleges which occupy the first ten places in terms of the percentage of teachers with research degrees are also among the first ten on the basis of title – student ratio. It is, however, difficult to establish a causal relationship between the two. One could argue that wherever there are teachers with better qualifications more and better books will be added to the library; one might also argue that the availability of a good library stimulates the academic interests of the teachers and induces them to do research. Undoubtedly there must always be an interaction between the two.

At the beginning of this chapter we noted that certain non-academic factors such as direct payment of salaries, unionisation of teachers, their engagement in other avocations, etc., have led to a general lowering of the standards of college education. Our analysis of the performance of the sample colleges, however, has shown that notwithstanding the general deterioration in standards, some colleges have been doing relatively better than others. The yardstick we adopted for the purpose was the percentage of pass in the university examinations at the predegree and the degree levels and the percentage of first class at the postgraduate level. Among the sample of 25 colleges we have seen that three colleges, namely Mar Ivanios, Bishop Moore and Mar Thoma maintained a level of performance above the sample average in all the three examinations – predegree, degree and postgraduate. Among the colleges which do not offer any postgraduate courses, Payyannur college and

Nirmalagiri have performed well in predegree and degree examinations. Among others, F.M.N., Quilon; St. Thomas, Trichur; and St. Paul's, Kalamasserry, have done well in the predegree and degree examinations, but not in examinations at the postgraduate level; S.N. College, Quilon and Catholicate College, Pathanamthitta, have a creditable record of results in the degree and postgraduate examinations but not in the predegree examination. These three categories together consisting of 10 colleges (40% of the sample) have attained different degrees of distinction in their performance in university examinations (We have left out those colleges which have done well in one examination only).

Financing and Performance

Our investigation has shown that out of the sample of 25 colleges, only eight do not insist on donations as a precondition for appointments or admissions. They consist of (1) Mar Ivanios, (2) Mar Thoma, (3) Fatima Mata National, (4) St. Paul's, (5) St. Thomas, (6) Nirmalagiri, (7) Bishop Moore and (8) St. Michael's. It is significant to note that all of them except St. Michael's have performed well in university examinations at two or more stages. Among the colleges which have done well in the university examinations, three, namely S.N. College, Quilon; Payyannur College, and Catholicate College, Pathanamthitta, receive donations for appointments and admissions. Among the 15 colleges with poor performance, all except St. Michael's are known to collect compulsory donations for appointments and admissions. The distribution of the sample colleges on the basis of performance and financing through compulsory donations is shown in Table 7.11.

While out of the eight colleges which do not accept compulsory donations three are outstanding, out of the 17 which do collect donations, none

TABLE 7.11: Performance and Financing of Sample Colleges

Level of performance	No. of colleges accepting compulsory donations	No. of colleges not accepting compulsory donations	Total
Outstanding	0	3	3
Very good	1	1	2
Good	2	3	5
Poor	14	1	15
Total	17	8	25

is outstanding. At the other end of the spectrum, among a total of 15 colleges with poor performance, all except one insist on donations. In between, among colleges with varying degrees of good performance, some collect compulsory donations while others do not. It is thus evident that the practice of collecting or not collecting donations as a precondition for appointments or admissions does not by itself lower or raise the quality of higher education. High levels of performance are shown by both colleges which do and which do not collect compulsory donations. However, the available evidence goes overwhelmingly against colleges accepting donations. While finance is essential for the development of the colleges, it does not mean that compulsory donations will have the desired effect. Apart from the immorality and illegality of compulsory donations, there is, from the practical point of view, a distinct possibility that instead of the entire amount collected being spent on the development of the college concerned, the whole amount or portions of it are diverted to non-academic purposes. It should be reiterated that adequate financial support is an essential precondition for the promotion of academic excellence. In all countries where private enterprise in the field of education is permitted, the most prestigious universities depend on voluntary giving in the form of unconditional donations and earmarked endowments for their sustenance and further growth. Such institutions, however, even in their wildest dreams, do not think of collecting compulsory donations from the faculty or students. It is the compulsory donations and not donations as such which are objectionable.

While finance is important for the improvement of the educational infrastructure of the colleges, compulsory donations are most likely to have a deleterious effect. Our interviews and dialogues with teachers do lend support to this contention. Teachers who obtain appointments on payment of donations are not found to be committed to their profession or loyal to the institution to the extent others are. Further, it is not unlikely that in cases in which donations are insisted on, the candidates who get appointed do not happen to be the best available. Similarly the students who are admitted on payment of capitation fees seldom happen to be the most eligible ones.

Generally speaking, colleges which hire the best teachers available and admit the most eligible students without being influenced by the prospects of donations find that the general public and the students' guardians are only too willing to help them in periods of financial crisis. Of course, as socio-economic conditions differ from one locality to another and from one community to another, a college in financial distress may not always succeed in raising through voluntary donations the entire amount it needs. A lasting solution to the problem of inadequate finances, it may be reiterated, is, in the face of mounting financial constraints on the budgets of the states, to permit colleges to charge higher tuition fees and other special fees and at the same time to safeguard the legitimate interests of the weaker sections by instituting a liberal scheme of scholarships. Instead of standardising the rates of tuition and other fees in private colleges, individual colleges may be permitted to vary their fees within certain prescribed limits. With rapidly rising costs of college education, the government is likely to find it increasingly difficult in the years to come to provide an adequate subsidy to the colleges. A rational system which provides for the generation of large internal financial resources should, therefore, be encouraged. Educational policy of the government should be geared up to this objective.

NOTES

1. It is learnt that the UGC has since discontinued the Faculty Improvement Programme.
2. While the predegree course constitutes the plus-two stage of the school education system in the rest of the country, it still forms part of the college system in Kerala. However, with the recent decision of the state government to implement the UGC scales of pay for college teachers in Kerala, steps are being taken to introduce the plus-two stage in the schools in a phased manner. The present predegree course which till now has been part of the university system is being delinked from the university though the predegree classes will continue to be housed in the present campuses for the time being.
3. Postgraduate teaching is confined to a few colleges. The small number of Ph.Ds among the faculty of the private colleges in the state seldom do research partly due to the inadequacy of laboratory and library facilities. Nevertheless, the presence of Ph.Ds on the faculty should be expected to have a toning-up effect on teaching. If it has, the effect should be reflected in the examination results.
4. Wilson College (Bombay), St. Stephen's (Delhi), St. John's (Agra), Madras Christian College (Madras), Hislop College (Nagpur) and Ewing Christian College (Allahabad) are some of the oldest and best known private colleges outside Kerala. Most of such colleges are well over hundred years old. It is pointed out that in these colleges more than half the faculty are Ph.Ds. For instance, Madras Christian College which completed 150 years in 1987 and had 72 Ph.Ds at the time distributed over 15 departments (an average of about 5 Ph. Ds per department).

8

SUMMARY AND CONCLUSIONS

Kerala stands in the forefront in the field of education among the states of the Indian Union. The literacy rate of Kerala (70.4%) is almost double that of the all-India average. In female literacy the state is far ahead (65.7%) of others. Such pre-eminence of the state is the outcome of a consistent policy followed in the past several decades of heavy public expenditure on education as indicated by its growth from Rs. 10 crores in 1957-58 to Rs. 489 crores in 1986-87. What is often overlooked, however, is the pioneering role played by private agencies in the field of education. To begin with, it was the western missionaries and the christian churches which came forward to establish schools of the modern type in the erstwhile princely states of Travancore and Cochin during the first half of the nineteenth century. At a much later stage, during the early decades of the twentieth century, other community-based social organisations such as the Sree Narayana Dharma Paripalana Yogam (formed in 1903) and the Nair Service Society (formed in 1914) also made their entry into the field of education.

Throughout the nineteenth century and almost the first half of the twentieth century, attention was concentrated by the state as well as private agencies on the extension of school education - primary and secondary. During this period ending 1947 a total of only 22 Arts and Science colleges came to be established in Kerala in the public and the private sectors together. The Zamorin's College, Calicut (1879); the C.M.S. College, Kottayam (1892); the Scott Christian College, Nagercoil; (1893); the Malabar Christian College, Calicut (1907); St. Thomas College, Trichur (1919); the Union Christian College, Alwaye (1921); and the St. Berchman's College, Changanacherry (1922) are some of the oldest colleges established in the private sector during this period. A period of rapid expansion of college education was heralded with the formation of the Kerala State in November 1956. The vast majority of the colleges started, however, continued to be in the private sector. This trend continued unabated till 1981 when there came about a sharp reversal of government policy. Thereafter priority was accorded to the public sector; out of 31 Arts and Science colleges founded during 1981-82, 22 colleges were those in the public sector. There are at present a total of 167 Arts and Science colleges in the State, out of which 132 are in the private sector.

The initial capital requirements of a newly-started college consists of a minimum prescribed extent of land, sufficient built-up space to accommodate the classes and the staff, and libraries and laboratories, according to accepted norms. The early history of colleges in Kerala has shown that there existed three ways of securing land for a college: (1) gift from the state government, (2) gifts from private individuals, and (3) purchase by management financed by donations from the public and the community under whose auspices the college was to be started. Funds for the construction of the buildings and the provision of other essential infrastructure have been by and large raised from the members of the communities concerned and the public. As regards subsequent capital requirements (needed for expansion) and the routine recurring expenditure, in addition to the sources already mentioned, the University Grants Commission has emerged as a major source. Needless to say, in this respect too the role played by private philanthropists has remained substantial. Among items of recurring expenditure, the most important is 'salaries' of the teaching and nonteaching staff.

The period prior to 1962 was one of almost complete financial autonomy for private colleges. The fees collected from students were retained by the colleges concerned and were used for payment of salaries of the staff and for meeting other expenses. In 1957, for the first time, the government announced uniform scales of pay for teachers in private and government colleges. In 1958 a modified scheme of UGC pay scales was introduced. Assistance from the UGC for payment of salaries to teachers in private colleges at the stipulated rates was promised only up to the end of 1961. The teachers insisted, however, that the enhanced scales of pay should continue beyond 1961 and launched an agitation. The Grant-in-Aid Code of 1962 was the direct outcome of this agitation. According to this Code, colleges were entitled to three different types of grants-in-aid, namely (i) teaching grants, (ii) building grants and (iii) equipment grants, according to certain prescribed norms. The Grant-in-Aid Code did not, however, resolve the longstanding conflict between the management and the teachers who accused the former of several malpractices. A major source of conflict was insecurity of tenure. Other issues related to retirement benefits, promotion of lecturers to the next higher grade on the basis of a minimum prescribed period of service, unification of fees in private colleges as well as between private and government colleges. At the end of a long-drawn agitation, the 'Direct Payment Agreement' was reached between the state government, the managements of colleges and the teachers' organisations. According to the terms and conditions of this Agreement, all educational agencies were to collect tuition fees only at the prescribed rates and remit the entire collection into the government treasury. The teaching and nonteaching staff were to be paid directly by the government. The colleges were also to receive certain grants such as contingency grant, maintenance grant, and library and laboratory grants according to norms prescribed. Further, all appointments to teaching and nonteaching posts and all admissions to courses of study were to be governed by certain uniform rules.

In the present study an attempt was made to (1) identify and evaluate the various sources of finance and the trends and patterns of financing, (2) evaluate the trends and patterns of expenditure against the goals of higher education and (3) discuss the relationship, if any, which exists between financing and academic performance as judged by the qualifications of teachers, examination results and other related criteria. Since there exist practically no published data on finances of private colleges, the required information was collected through a sample survey of 25 Arts and Science colleges which forms 19 per cent of the colleges in the private sector. Care was taken to make the sample representative by taking into account the regional specificities and the differences in the type of management. The data pertain to the period 1972-73 to 1985-86.

The different sources of finance for colleges in the private sector have been grouped under two categories: institutional and non-institutional. Among the sources of institutional finance, the state government is the most prominent. Government grant per college increased from Rs. 2.23 lakhs in 1972-73 to Rs. 26.98 lakhs in 1985-86. The level of financial support by the state government has consistently remained at over 90 per cent of the total. Among the other institutional sources, the University Grants Commission and the college managements are the important ones. While the average grant per sample college from the UGC increased from Rs. 11,375 in 1972-73 to Rs. 1.59 lakhs in 1985-86, the corresponding amounts received from the managements were Rs. 6,112 and Rs. 40,786 respectively. Grants from the university to which the college is affiliated has remained too meagre at below 1 per cent.

As regards the grants received from the state government, those for salaries are by far the most important. The average grant for salaries (of teaching and nonteaching staff) per sample college increased from Rs. 2.16 lakhs in 1972-73 to 26.47 lakhs in 1985-86. The Direct Payment Agreement entered into with the managements of colleges and teachers' organisations has proved to be a heavy financial burden to the state government. Next in importance to grants for payment of salaries comes scholarships and stipends. The average grant per sample college for this item increased from Rs. 5,821 in 1972-73 to Rs. 41,233 in 1985-86. During the same period, its share in total grants declined from 2.6 per cent to 1.5 per cent. The remaining four types of grants namely library, laboratory, maintenance and contingency, constituted less than one per cent of the total. For the entire 14-year period under review, the average annual government grant per sample college for library came to a mere Rs. 534 and that for laboratories was only Rs. 1,168.

As the tuition fees collected by the colleges are remitted into the government treasury, the gross amount disbursed by the government by way of grants does not constitute the actual burden to the government. The burden is represented by the difference between total grants and total receipts from tuition fees. Tuition fees collected from students have generally formed less than 18 per cent of the grants provided by the government. While government grants (for eleven colleges for which complete data were available) per sample college increased from Rs. 11.42 lakhs in 1976-77 to Rs. 27.78 lakhs in 1985-86 registering more than 143 per cent increase, tuition fees increased from Rs. 2.04 lakhs to Rs. 3.67 lakhs showing less than 80 per cent increase. Tuition fees prevailing in Kerala are one of the lowest in the whole country.

Eventhough the state government shoulders the major responsibility for financing the recurring expenditures of the private colleges, government grants often fall short of the requirements of individual colleges. In such situations, the managements concerned make attempts to supplement them. During the period from 1972-73 to 1985-86 relatively large amounts were provided by the managements for purchase of land and construction of buildings. In certain years, the average amount per sample college was as high as, or more than, Rs. 50,000. Next to land and buildings, financial support for laboratories was a major item of assistance extended by managements.

The role of the University Grants Commission has steadily expanded in recent years. The average amount of UGC grant per sample college increased from Rs. 11,375 in 1972-73 to Rs. 158,843 in 1985-86. Among the various purposes for which assistance was received, construction of buildings was the most important. UGC assistance per sample college for this item increased from Rs.3,961 in 1972-73 to Rs.56,425 in 1985-86. Next in importance was the assistance given for purchase of books and journals; the average amount per sample colleges rose from Rs.2,771 in 1972-73 to Rs. 4,0971 in 1985-86.

The University to which the college is affiliated is seen to account for only very negligible part in the amounts or patterns of financing. The very limited flow of funds taking place from the University to the colleges consists of (1) university merit scholarships and (2) grants for National Service Scheme.

Non-institutional finance for private colleges

consists of fees other than tuitions fees, donations and certain miscellaneous items. Receipts per sample college from this source increased from Rs. 89,019 in 1972-73 to Rs. 226,799 in 1985-86. Of the three types of non-institutional finance, fees (excluding tuitions fees) have accounted for the bulk of the receipts throughout the period under review. The average receipts per college from this source increased from Rs. 45,750 in 1972-73 to Rs. 177,146 in 1985-86. Five types of fees, namely caution deposit, games fee, laboratory fee, admission fee, and magazine and calendar fees together account for over one-half of the total amount collected under this head.

Donations received by the colleges come from (a) teaching and nonteaching staff, (b) students and/or parents, and (c) general public. While the average amount of donations from the staff per sample college varied from Rs. 511 in 1975-76 to Rs. 3,340 in 1981-82, in most years such donations formed less than one-fifth of the total under the head. On the other hand, donations from students and/or parents and the general public have remained far more important. The average amount of donations per sample college from students and/or parents varied from Rs.525 in 1975-76 to Rs. 21,085 in 1983-84 and its relative share varied between 6.3 per cent in 1980-81 and 71.5 per cent in 1972-73. The corresponding figures for donations from the public were Rs. 235 in 1977-78 and Rs. 69,712 in 1984-85; they ranged between 7.3 per cent (in 1972-73) and 89.5 per cent in (1980-81). It is highly doubtful that all these donations were in the nature of voluntary payments. Among the miscellaneous sources of receipts, 'borrowings' was the most important. However, it is seen that the role of borrowing has been on the decline from Rs. 37,399 (98.5%) in 1972-73 to Rs.14,081 (78.3%) in 1985-86.

Since the accounts of the private colleges are

subjected to audit by the government, it is most likely that the major share of the donations are not shown as such in the accounts of the sample colleges, but are received direct by managements and left unaccounted in college records. Further, donations received for appointment of teachers and admission of students are, if at all, shown as donations from the public for purposes such as construction of additional buildings, development of library, etc. It was found that, of the sample of 25 colleges, all except 8 colleges collected 'compulsory' donations as a precondition for appointment of teachers. In terms of the amounts of donations currently collected per appointment the sample colleges which follow the practice were classified into three categories : low (Rs. 25,000 to Rs. 40,000), medium (Rs.40,000 to Rs. 55,000) and high (Rs. 55,000 to Rs.75,000). Seven colleges belonged to the 'low' group, five to the 'medium' group and another five to the 'high' groups.

Managements of colleges are known to collect also donations from candidates for admissions to different courses of study under the 'management quota'. Such donations vary in amount with the level of the course (Predegree, degree or postgraduate) and the subject/discipline. Out of the 25 sample colleges, 15 colleges collect donations for admissions. Generally speaking, colleges which collect donations for appointments also collect donations for admissions. For the predegree course donation per student varied from less than Rs.300 to Rs. 1,500; science groups attract the largest donations and arts groups the lowest. At the degree level, it varied from Rs. 500 to Rs. 7,000, science subjects such as physics and chemistry accounting for the highest donations and humanities like philosophy, history and politics the lowest. For admission to postgraduate courses, the range of capitation fee was between Rs. 6,000 and Rs. 15,000. While the number of vacancies of teachers arising each year would be very limited (less than half a dozen) and vary much from year to year, the number of students admitted under the management quota might run to a few hundreds and not vary from year to year. Hence, for the colleges which collect capitation fees, though the donation per student may be relatively very small, the total amount received would be quite substantial. The question, however, remains whether the entire funds thus raised are used for meeting the legitimate needs of the college. It is evident beyond doubt that those colleges/managements which supplement their financial resources with compulsory donations – assuming that the entire donations are channelised to college funds – would not suffer from any financial stringency; on the contrary, they might even command surplus funds. For others there might arise a financial crunch. Larger grants from the state government, higher rates of tuition fees/special fees, and delinking of the colleges, if feasible, from the 'Direct Payment Scheme', in a carefully phased manner are some of the remedies which could be thought of.

In addition to identifying and evaluating the various sources of institutional and non-institutional finance for colleges in the private sector in Kerala, an attempt was made to discuss also their expenditures. The average capital expenditure (such as those on Purchase and Improvement of Land, Construction of Buildings, Installation of Laboratory equipment, Purchase of Books and Periodicals, etc.) per sample college registered a significant increase from Rs. 26,189 in 1972-73 to Rs. 134,211 in 1985-86. As regards capital expenditure on different items, expenditure per sample college on building construction increased from Rs. 11,316 in 1972-73 to Rs. 47,914 in 1985-86, its relative share varying from 7 per cent in 1981-82 to 66.5 per cent in 1974-75. The next important item of capital expenditure is laboratory equipment; average expenditure per sample college on this item increased from Rs. 4,335 (16.5%) in 1972-73 to Rs. 38,670 (28.8%) in 1985-86. During the same period the average expenditure on library rose from Rs. 5,258 in 1972-73 to Rs. 30,019 in 1985-86 (20.1% to 22.6%). A few sample colleges, however, had a consistently high record of capital expenditure.

As regards recurring expenditure, the average amount per sample college increased from Rs. 24,334 in 1972-73 to Rs. 66,473 in 1985-86. Among the different items of recurring expenditure, repairs and maintenance is the most important; expenditure on this rose from Rs. 5,319 (21.9%) in 1972-73 to Rs. 19,198 (28.9%) in 1985-86. Since maintenance grants are not received from the government promptly, several colleges have not undertaken maintenance of buildings on a regular basis. The next most important item of recurring expenditure is Purchase of Chemicals and Materials for the Laboratories; the average expenditure per sample college on this item increased from Rs. 5,551 (22.8%) in 1972-73 to Rs.15,495 (23.3%) in 1985-86. As laboratory fees collected from the students are insufficient to meet the full cost of chemicals and materials used, some colleges depend on their Parent-Teacher, Associations for additional funds. An item of recurring expenditure of growing importance is Sports and Games. Over the years a steady increase in the expenditure on this item is noted in absolute as well as relative terms. Thus the average annual recurring expenditure per sample college on sports and games increased from Rs. 3,534 (14.5%) in 1972-73 to Rs. 13,987 (21%) in 1985-86. In fact a few colleges have been spending exceptionally large amounts varying from Rs. 22,651 to Rs. 40,632 on this item. It may, however, be noted that what is indicated as recurring expenditure on sports and games may, in fact, be capital expenditure - a problem identical to the one we confronted in relation to expenditure on laboratories.

Our analysis of the expenditure of the sample colleges has shown that net of payment of salaries of the staff-teaching and nonteaching - most colleges spend only paltry sums on the upkeep of the institutions; the accent is on survival and not on development.

After analysing the various sources of finance of the colleges and the pattern of their expenditures, we attempted an evaluation of the performance of the sample colleges. It was noted that the deterioration that had set in the field of higher education was the outcome of certain developments that had been steadily taking place over the years such as unionisation of teachers, growth of multiple unions of teachers, introduction of time-bound promotions of teachers and teachers' engagement in other avocations. In spite of the general deterioration in standards it was noted that some colleges have been performing much better than others. The academic performance of the colleges was sought to be evaluated on the basis of their pass-percentage in university examinations - predegree, degree and postgraduate. Colleges where broadly divided into two groups using average percentage of pass (for postgraduate examinations average percentage of first class) for the sample as the cut-off point, colleges having pass-percentage (or percentage of first class in respect of postgraduate examinations) below the sample average being treated as poor performers while those with higher percentages were treated as good performers. It was found that while some colleges did well in all the three examinations, namely predegree, degree and postgraduate, there were others which did well in two only - predegree and degree or degree and postgraduate. (colleges which did well only in one examination were not treated as good performers). In all, there were 10 such colleges in the sample of 25. Among the specific factors which contributed to the superior performance of these institutions, we identified two, namely quality of teachers as measured by the percentage of teachers with research degrees, and library facilities as measured by the title-student ratio. It was also observed that among the ten colleges with above-average performance, three colleges received compulsory donations for appointment of teachers and/or admission of students; and out of the 15 colleges with poor performance as many as 14 collected donations. While finance is very important for development of a college, finance in the form of compulsory donations often does not help. Apart from the immorality and illegality of the practice, it is highly doubtful whether the entire amount thus collected is in fact spent for the intended purpose. Also appointment of teachers and admission of students on payment of donations have a demoralising effect on the academic atmosphere of a college. With the worsening financial scenario confronting the state government, a lasting solution to the problem of inadequate college finances would be to effect a rational restructuring of tuition and other fees with adequate safeguards to protect the interests of students belonging to weaker sections.

INDEX

Academic excellence, 16
    objectives, 147
Admission fee, 85-86
Affiliating system, 76
Affiliation, 42
Agitation, 41, 46, 151
Agra, 26
Agreement, 46, 47, 49, 151
Ajith, V.S., 6
Alleppey, 25
All Kerala Private College Teachers Association (AKPCTA), 126
Annual donation, 92
    government grant, 63
    tuition fee, 43, 64
Arts and science colleges, 17
Asan, Kumaran, 26
Ashruf, K., 6
Association fee, 81
Autonomy, 39 151

Backward communities, 48
Bailey, Benjamin, 15, 22
Basel German Mission, 23
Benaras, 26
Bishop Moore College, 92, 136
Bombay, 26
Borrowings, 94
Brennen, E., 23

Calicut, 75
    Guruvayurappan College, 23
Cannanore, 28
Capital expenditures, 37, 109
Capitation fees, 102, 103, 157
    payment of, 147
Catholics, 28
Catholicate college, 75
Changanacherry, 36, 37
Chelannur, Sree Narayana educational society, 35
Christians, 26, 28
    churches, 14, 37, 98, 105
Church Missionary Society (CMS), 15, 22, 34
Cochin, 54
Colleges education financing of, 33
    expenditures of, 108
    financing evolution of, 33
        problems of, 160
    institutional financing of, 54
    level education expansion of, 24
    performance of, 128-29
College union fees, 81
Compulsory donations, 92, 96, 145, 146, 157, 160
Constraints, 147
Contingency grant, 49
Criticism, 16, 30, 38
Cutchery (court), 35

Data, 17, 54, 104
Degree examinations, 135, 145
    results of, 132
Deterioration, 159
Direct Payment Agreement, 33, 38, 46, 47, 48, 49, 50, 53, 60, 67, 71, 81, 107, 125, 151, 153
    financial provision of, 49
Disciplines, 98, 99
Donations, 16, 19, 34, 36, 38, 81,

82, 85, 87, 89, 108, 145, 155
categories, 97
colleges collect, 99
increasing role of, 94
pre-degree course, 100
voluntary, 921
way of, 95
Donations for admissions, 99
Donations for teachers, 96

East India Company, 21
Economy, 25
Education, public expenditure on, 149-50
Educational agencies, 6, 47, 48, 94
endeavours, 5
infrastructure, 15
systems, 26
Examination results, 128
Ezhavas, 15, 26, 28

Faculty Improvement Programmes (FIP), 72, 127, 139
quality of, 138
Fees, 82-85
Financial,
assistance, 76
analysis of, 57-58
operations, 40
problems, 105
sources of, 80-82

Games fee, 81, 85
Generalisation, 18-19
Gopa Kumar, B., 6
Gopinathan Nair, P.R., 7
Government grants, 57, 60
net grants, 64
Grant-in-aid code, 41-43, 46-49, 67, 151
implementation of, 44
scheme of, 15, 44
Guruvayurappan College, 89, 101

Harijans, 61
Haryana, 13
High-level committee, 16
Higher education, community for, 106
financing of, 6
goals of, 16
report on, 67
standards of, 103

Indian Council of Social Science Research (ICSSR), 6
Indian Union, 149
Initial capital expenditures, 33
Institutional finance, sources of, 77

Jagannathan, K., 6

Kerala,
Arts and science colleges in, 28
development college education in, 21-22
economy, 13
public expenditure, 14
university, 26
Kottayam, C.M.S. College, 23, 34
Kumara Pillai Commission Report (KPCR), 60

Laboratory fee, 85
Liberalisation, 60
Library facilities, 16, 142, 160
Library and laboratory grants, 50
Loan, 94
Lucknow, 26

Madhavan, T.K., 26
Madras Christian College, 25
Madras University, 21
Magazine and calendar fee, 81
Maharaja's college, 23, 24
Mahatma Gandhi, 131, 134
Mahatma Gandhi College, 27, 34, 35
Maintenance grant, 50
Malabar region, 17, 131
Malabar Christian College, 24
Malankara Orthodox Syrian

Church (MOSC), 98
Malpractices, 151
Management, 33, 37, 42, 46, 57, 68, 71, 81, 98, 105, 126, 143, 156
Mannath, Padmanabhan, 26
Mar Ivanios, 136
Mar Thoma Church, 105, 136
Mathew, K.C., 7
Mead, C., 22
Medical examination, 81
Munro, Colonel, 21
Muslim Educational Society (MES), 18, 29, 67

Nagam Aiya, V., 21
Nagercoil seminary, 22
Nairs, 26, 28
Nair Service Society (NSS), 5, 15, 26, 36, 67
National Cadet Core (NCC), 77
Nirmalagiri, 144
Non-academic factors, 144
Non-budgetary sources, 15-16
Non-financial factors, 124
Non-institutional finance, 157
  types of, 155-56
Non-institutional sources, 83
Non-teaching staff, 43
  allowances, 49
  grant, 44-45
  salaries, 19, 49, 60-61, 91

Obligation, 77
Old Seminary (Syrian College), 34
Open-merit quota, 98
Organisations, 35, 55

Palghat, Victoria college, 23
Palpu, T., 26
Panchamukhi, P.R., 7
Pandalam, 36
Parent-teachers Associations, 158
Perunal (religious festivals), 37
Policy, 30
Political affiliations, 126
  parties, 61
  sympathies, 126
Postgraduate courses, 100, 135
  examinations, 136, 159
Prakash, V., 6
Predegree classes, 79
  examination results, 129, 134
Private Arts and Science college, 39
Private colleges, finances of, 17-18, 46-47
  institutional financing, 55
  management of, 89
  non-institutional finance for, 154
  teachers' association, 126
Private educational management, 5
Private sector, 14, 15, 30, 150
  colleges in, 80
    financing of, 53-54, 108-109
    prestigious in, 139-40
Proliferation, 125
Provident fund, 49
Public sector, 6, 124, 150
Punjab, 13

Quilon, 27, 28, 35, 75, 145
  F.M.N. college, 96
  Sree Narayana college, 119

Ramachandran, R., 6
Ramaswamy, C.P., 27
Rani Laxshmi Bai, 34
Raveendran, C., 6
Recurring expenditures, 37, 38, 43, 109, 114, 116, 120, 158
  different items of, 116
Reservation, 42
Retirement benefits, 46, 50
Ringletaube, William Tobias, 14

Salaries, 19, 39, 41, 49, 60, 61, 124
  payments of, 122, 151
Sample college,
  capital expenditure, 113
  distribution of, 18
  financial assistance, 69, 73
  recurring expenditure, 120

Sanatana Vidyasala, 27
Scheduled Castes and Tribes, 106
Scholarships, 61-62
Scott Christian College, 22
Second World War, 25
Sivarama Krishna Iyer, V.S., 35
Sixth Five Year Plan, 72
Sree Narayana Dharma
    Paripalana Yogam (SNDP), 5, 15, 18, 26, 27, 149
Sree Narayana Trust, 67
St. Thomas college, 24
State Government grants, 58
State Pay Commission, 54
Stipends, 61, 62
Syrian Church, 21, 22

Teachers, engagement of, 127
    inter-departmental
        distribution of, 141
    multiple unions of, 126
    organisations, 61
    unionisation of, 125
Teaching grants, 42-43
Thirumulpad, P.M., 35
Thomas, Joy, 6
Time-bound promotion, 127
Tiruvalla, Mar Thana College, 96
Titus, C.T., 6
Travancore, 5, 14
    State manual, 21
    university, 26, 27
Trivandrum, 22
Tuition fees, 39, 41, 66, 82, 86, 151, 153

Ulpanna Pirivu, 36
Unemployment, 62
Union Christian College, 25, 35
Unionisation, 62
University examination, 136, 159
University Grants Commission
    (UGC), 38, 41, 53, 57, 63, 71, 79, 127, 152, 154

Vidyasala, 23
Vocational education, 29
Voluntary donations, 101, 147

Women's education, 13

Zamorin's Guruvayurappan
    College, 23